CHOSEN IN CHRIST?

Chosen in Christ?

A dialogue concerning free will and
human responsibility as they relate to the
redemptive purposes of our sovereign God.

by

James L Crookes

JOHN RITCHIE LTD
CHRISTIAN PUBLICATIONS

40 Beansburn, Kilmarnock, Scotland

ISBN 1 904064 27 2

Typeset by John Ritchie Ltd., Kilmarnock
Printed by Bell & Bain

Contents

Abbreviations

ASV	American Standard Version
A to Q	Answers to Questions
AV	Authorised Version
F & M	Forster and Marston
GNB	Good News Bible (Today's English Version)
HDB	Hastings Dictionary of the Bible
KJV	King James Version
Moffatt	James Moffatt; A New Translation of the Bible
NEB	New English Bible
NIV	New International Version
NT	New Testament
OT	Old Testament
p., pp.	page, pages
Phillips	J.B. Phillips; The NT in Modern English
RSV	Revised Standard Version

Acknowledgements

I wish to express my thanks and acknowledge my indebtedness to publishers, literary agents and authors for the kind permissions to use copyright material as follows:

from *Hastings Dictionary of the Bible*, published by T & T Clark, Edinburgh;

from *Commentary on the New Testament*, by Professor E M Blaiklock, 1977, publishers Hodder & Stoughton, copyright permission from Edward England Books, Literary Agent;

from *The New International Version of the Bible*, published by Hodder and Stoughton;

from *A New Translation of the Bible*, by Dr James Moffatt, published by Hodder and Stoughton;

from *The Tyndale New Testament Commentary: Matthew*, by R V G Tasker, published by IVP (Tyndale Press London, 1971 ed.);

from *The Tyndale New Testament Commentary: Romans*, by F F Bruce, published by IVP (Leicester 1983);

from *The Tyndale Old Testament Commentary: Exodus*, by R Alan Cole, published by IVP (Tyndale Press London, 1973 ed.);

from *The Acts of the Apostles*, by G Campbell Morgan, published by Pickering and Inglis Ltd., London 1965 (Permission from Marshall Pickering);

from *The Gospel According to Matthew*, by G Campbell Morgan, published by Marshall, Morgan and Scott, London, 1976 ed. (Permission from Marshall Pickering);

from *The Gospel According to John*, by G Campbell Morgan, published by Marshall, Morgan and Scott, London 1976 (Permission from Marshall Pickering);

from *This Was His Faith* (Expository Letters of G Campbell Morgan, compiled and edited by Jill Morgan), published by Pickering and Inglis, London n.d. (Permission from Marshall Pickering);

from *Searchlights from the Word*, by G Campbell Morgan, published by Marshall, Morgan and Scott, London 1976 (Permission from Marshall Pickering);

from *The Pickering Bible Commentary*, published by Pickering and Inglis, 1984 ed. (Permission from Marshall Pickering);

from *The Wycliffe Bible Commentary*, published by Oliphants 1963 (Permission from Marshall Pickering);

from *The Revised Standard Version of the Bible*, copyright 1946, 1952, 1971 by the Division of Christian Education of the National Council of the Churches of Christ in the USA. Used by permission;

from *The New Scofield Reference Bible*, published by Oxford University Press, New York;

from *The New English Bible*, 2nd ed. 1970, published by the Oxford and Cambridge Presses;

from *Answers to Questions*, by Professor F F Bruce, published by Paternoster Press, Exeter, 1972.

In addition to the above list I received personal grants of permission from living authors, which I greatly appreciate. I express my gratitude to Dr J Sidlow Baxter for his kind permission to quote from *Explore the Book*, published by Zondervan Publishing House, Grand Rapids, Michigan 1975; and to Mr Roger Forster, whom I have the pleasure of knowing personally, for his unrestricted permission to use material from *God's Strategy in Human History*, by Roger Forster and V. Paul Marston (Published by Send The Light Trust, Bromley, Kent, 1973 ed., and in the USA by Tyndale House Publishers, Wheaton, Illinois, 1974). Readers will observe the extensive use I have made of this important book, but I would add that it was the insights gained from it which started me off to write this work. I am most grateful for that helpful impetus, and I gladly acknowledge my indebtedness.

Finally, I record my thanks to members of my family for their great help to me: to David, for important stylistic suggestions and improvements, and for his careful vetting of the script, and to Danny and Helen for assisting and instructing me in the use of the computer. Their help was invaluable, and I am glad to put it on record.

I also acknowledge the help of Dr Bert Cargill in bringing the manuscript into its present format for publication.

Introduction

Recently I received a tract which bears the title, 'DID CHRIST DIE FOR YOU?' The thrust of its message is that Christ died for the 'Elect' only. It is issued by a Christian Fellowship whose creed denies that man has free will. This is a deterministic creed based only on *selected* proof-texts; one which does not take into account *all* that the Scriptures reveal to us about the purposes of God and the sacrificial death of our great Saviour, the Lord Jesus Christ.

This essay aims to be a helpful response to that tract by setting out some of the great 'universal' texts of Scripture. But it is also necessary to deal with those verses in the Bible which on surface reading do seem to be deterministic. I have attempted to show that they do not support determinism at all. I have structured this essay in dialogue form as a series of discussions between two fictitious people, a student (CAL), and a mature Christian (JAY).

I write from the position that where there is no free will there can be no responsibility, and where there is no responsibility there can be neither praise nor censure, neither reward nor punishment. I take that as axiomatic, and it should be recognized as being so, so long as we keep in mind that free will in this context refers only to the God-given power of moral choice.

It is true that man is "dead in transgressions and sins", but that is spiritual death - separation from God. He is not morally dead. Freedom of the will has meaning only in reference to the moral nature of man. While we admit the prevalence of habit, the influence of environment and the power of genetic inheritance, Scripture compels us to acknowledge that there is such a thing as responsibility. Indeed, what makes a man human is the fact that he is a responsible being, even though responsibility may be diminished by mental or physical illness or disease. He is not a mere machine. When we view this truth in the light of God who is Sovereign and Omniscient, difficulties do arise for our minds. This will be discussed in the essay.

Up to this point in the Introduction, I have had only theological determinism in view, but I have already mentioned the power of genetic inheritance as one of the influences in life. Some scientists hold to an extreme form of genetic determinism which denies any possibility of human free will at all. So, because some young Christians may encounter difficulty in rebutting this extreme theory, I shall digress to include it for a brief consideration in Discussion Six.

At the outset, I wish to disclaim any originality in what I write in this essay, because in a long lifetime of reading and preparing for meetings and for conversational Bible Readings, I must have absorbed much from very many writers which has now so entered into my own thought that it lodges there as my own. As C S Lewis has said, "Facts and inferences, and even turns of expression, find a lodging in a man's mind, he scarcely remembers how." Wherever this is recognized by a reader of these pages to be so in my case, I trust it will be understood, but I shall quote sources where I am able to do so, many of which are listed in my Acknowledgements.

James L. Crookes
Belfast

For whom did Christ die?

JAY: Come in, Cal. You wanted to discuss something with me. I see you have a notebook and a sheaf of notes. What's the problem?

CAL: Yes, I need some help. I've been given a tract, entitled "Did Christ die for you?" It says that Christ did not die for everyone, but only for those who were given to Him by His heavenly Father. Here is the tract. Have you come across this notion?

JAY: Yes. Indeed I have some knowledge of the people who produced the tract. They are good earnest Christians, but they do have extreme views which I regard as unscriptural. They do not believe that men and women have any free will, for instance. Curiously enough, the tract asks you to think about the texts, "For God sent not His Son into the world to condemn the world, but that the world through Him might be saved. He that believeth on Him is not condemned; but he that believeth not is condemned already because he hath not believed in the name of the only-begotten Son of God." (John 3:17, 18).

CAL: Are you saying, 'curiously enough' because these verses seem to contradict their restrictive statement? It is *the world* that is in view, not a restricted few, and it is clear that there is a responsibility to believe, I think. Yet there is one verse which might seem to support their restrictive view. It is Eph 5:25: "Christ loved the Church and gave Himself for it."

JAY: I agree that there is a responsibility to believe. Professor

Bruce was once asked about the Scripture which you have just quoted: "Is it more Scriptural to say that Christ died for His people (the elect) or that He died for all?" He answered, "To say that He died for His people is certainly Scriptural (Eph. 5:25), but it is equally Scriptural to say that He died for all; as it states in 1 Tim 2:6 - He 'gave Himself as a ransom for all, the testimony to which was borne at the proper time'. And when Scripture says 'all' in a context like that it means 'all'.

"Some people who are not sure of this statement may find it profitable to consider certain exegetical comments of John Calvin. On Matthew 26:28 and Mark 14:24 ("which is shed for many"), he says:

'By the word MANY he means not a part of the world only, but the whole human race.'

As for Luke 22:20 ("which is poured out for you"), this reminds believers to apply to themselves personally what has been provided for all. He says:

'Let us not only remember in general that the world has been redeemed by the blood of Christ, but let each one consider for himself that his own sins have been expiated thereby.'

Again, on Rom. 5:18 ("the free gift came unto all men to justification of life"), he says:

'Paul makes grace common to all men, not in fact because it extends to all, but because it is offered to all.'

And he shows what he means by saying that it does not extend to all, in the words which immediately follow:

'Although Christ suffered for the sins of the world and is offered by the goodness of God without distinction to all men, yet not all receive Him.' " (p.197 A to Q)

Now that is a long quotation, but I give it firstly because Bruce, who called himself 'an impenitent Augustinian and Calvinist' [1], cites John Calvin, but more importantly because he expresses the Scriptural truth. Eph 5:25 is no more 'restrictive' than is Gal 2:20 where Paul could claim, "the Son of God, who loved me, and gave Himself for me".

But let us turn to some other Scriptures which teach the truth of

God's plan of redemption. You know that salvation is not universal, because it requires a response. But the price has been paid for all; salvation is available for all who will believe. Start with John 3:16, which the tract omitted.

CAL: "For God so loved the WORLD, that He gave His only begotten Son, that WHOSOEVER believeth in Him should not perish, but have everlasting life." There again it is 'the world' that is in view, and life is offered to 'whosoever believeth.' Isn't that so?

JAY: Surely. I'll ask you to turn to a number of other texts, but keeping first to John's Gospel, we have the testimony of John the Baptist (1:29), "Behold the Lamb of God, which taketh away the sin of the WORLD", and in 6:51 we read our Lord's own words, "I am the living bread which came down from heaven. If ANYONE eats of this bread, he will live for ever. The bread is my flesh, which I will give for the life of the WORLD." Now turn please to 1 Tim. 2:4.

CAL: It reads that God "wants ALL men to be saved and to come to the knowledge of the truth".

JAY: You may remember also Titus 2:11 which says: "For the grace of God that brings salvation has appeared to ALL men." But repentance is necessary.

CAL: Paul does stress in Acts 17:30, that "God now commandeth ALL men everywhere to repent".

JAY: Yes, and Peter points out (2 Pet. 3:9), "God is not willing that ANY should perish, but that ALL should come to repentance." Perhaps at this point I should say that I'm not going into a theological discussion. We may have to do that later when we consider your list of texts. I simply want the Scriptures themselves to reveal the universal aspect of the love of God, of His grace and mercy in Christ Jesus, and to emphasise that God views us as responsible creatures. He requires a response to His gracious offer of salvation.

CAL: And so He "commands all men everywhere to repent..."

JAY: Yes. I see you've been taking notes. Well, here are more Scriptures to read. Turn up 2 Cor. 5:14.

CAL: Here it is. "For Christ's love compels us, because we are convinced that One died for ALL."

JAY: That's right, and further down the chapter, verse 19, we read (in the NIV) that "God was reconciling the WORLD to Himself in Christ." Shall I leave off now, or do you want me to quote further Scriptures?

CAL: If you've any more references maybe you'd let me have them now. Then I'll bring up those Scriptures which seem to favour the determinist approach.

JAY: All right. Look at 1 John 2:2. "He is the propitiation for our sins: and not for ours only, but also for the sins of the WHOLE WORLD." And in 4:14, 15 John says, "We have seen and do testify that the Father sent the Son to be the Saviour of the WORLD."

CAL: That could not be clearer, could it?

JAY: We agree on that, though there are other people who would not. Here's another great truth from Heb 2:9. "But we see Jesus, who was made a little lower than the angels for the suffering of death, crowned with glory and honour; that He by the grace of God should taste death for EVERY man."

CAL: That clearly focuses on the individual, doesn't it? I have a note here of two other Scriptures, one in Rom 10:13, "Whosoever shall call upon the name of the Lord shall be saved." 'Whosoever' has no restrictions on it. The other one is from Isa 45:22. "Look unto Me and be ye saved, all the ends of the earth."

JAY: Those two verses are very appropriate.

CAL: The sheaf of notes you see me with contains a number of texts which puzzle me, and I have brought them for your comments. May I mention two of them before we finish this discussion?

JAY: Go ahead. What is your first one?

CAL: I have Acts 2:47 jotted down: "And the Lord added to the church daily such as should be saved." Isn't that clear? "Such as should be saved"?

JAY: You are quoting the AV which unfortunately gives an inaccurate translation there. There is no real problem in the verse at all. If you consult modern translations you will find that it should rather read "the Lord added to their number daily those who were being saved" or "those whom He was saving". That should clear your difficulty there. The only thing I would add is that we don't 'join' the Church, though we may become members of a local church or fellowship. It is God who adds us to the Church.

CAL: You've cleared up that text for me, but I should have brought up verse 23 first. Could we go back to it now? "Him, being delivered by the determinate counsel and foreknowledge of God, ye have taken, and by wicked hands have crucified and slain." Other translations agree with the AV here, don't they?

JAY: Yes indeed. Here we are on holy ground. Our verse tells us that the Cross was no accident, no contingency plan. Our Lord Jesus Christ is the Lamb of God foreordained before the foundation of the world. The Cross is in the eternal plan of God and He made His plans in the light of what would happen, if I may put it in those human terms. His plan to deliver up His Son to them was made in the knowledge that they would crucify Him.

CAL: But His enemies and Judas, weren't they doing what they had to do?

JAY: No; not at all. God did not determine their wickedness. He used it in His divine overruling as always. Nothing is said to minimise the guilt of His enemies. THEY put the Lord Jesus to death; God knew that would happen and He delivered Him up to them in that foreknowledge. They alone did the act and they were responsible for it.

CAL: That verse does seem to me to be one of the boldest presentations of the paradox of divine predestination and human free will.

JAY: Paradox perhaps, but not contradiction. It illustrates or reveals God's strategy for the ultimate health of the universe through His Son as the Lamb of God. He does not meet violence with like force but overcomes evil with good.

CAL: My next text is Acts 13:48. It reads, "And when the Gentiles heard this, they were glad, and glorified the word of the Lord: and as many as were ordained to eternal life believed." I confess that seems to be insurmountable: "as many as were ordained to eternal life believed". That statement is clear, isn't it?

JAY: That is not, however, the meaning of the original Greek. One Greek scholar gives this comment. "The Jews had already of their own choice rejected Christ. Among the Gentiles they found 'those who set themselves in place for eternal life'." This correctly renders a middle verb (in this tense middle and passive coincide). 'Ordained' of course, is not theologically loaded. It meant 'set in place' in the English of the time." [2]

CAL: I haven't studied Greek. What is meant by a middle verb?

JAY: You know that an English verb has two voices, active and passive. In the active voice the subject does an action; in the passive voice the subject has something done to it. Greek, in many verbs, has another voice called the middle voice, in which the subject both acts and is acted upon; that is, the subject acts directly or indirectly on itself. It has been explained in this way: 'The middle voice chiefly signifies that a person has a special interest in the effects of the action, that he is acting either upon,

17

or for, himself, or that when he is acting for others he has a personal interest in their condition or welfare.' The grammar of the middle voice is complex and no simple rule can be given in respect of it. The context is very important in deciding the meaning, but perhaps that generalised explanation will help you.

CAL: I understand your explanation, but it radically alters the meaning of the text for me.

JAY: Well, look at it now in its context. In the background to the verse there are two very different groups in the conflict. On the one hand are men 'filled with jealousy', and on the other hand are Gentiles 'filled with gladness'. On the one hand are those who 'contradicted the things that were spoken...and blasphemed'; on the other hand were those who 'glorified the word of God'. Then we come to another contrast: on the one side are those who 'counted themselves unworthy of eternal life', and on the other side are those who 'set themselves in place for eternal life'. The Scriptures there are consistent. Does that make the meaning clear?

CAL: Yes, I see that now. So the word 'ordained' in the text has no reference to any direct act or decree of God. It refers to the result of the attitude of the men who, in faith, took their place as repentant sinners.

JAY: It does. So we see that some 'blasphemed' while others 'believed'. This set of contrasts reveals the conflict and division following the preaching of the Word. It reveals also the responsibility of the hearers. [3]

CAL: Could we break off now please? All this is helpful for me and I have made some notes, but I would like to assimilate it all before we go on.

JAY: All right. But let me end this discussion with Paul's answer to the question, 'For whom did Christ die?' Look at Romans 5:6: "Christ died for the ungodly." That takes in everybody, all of us, God be praised! But there must be the believing response to the divine love and sacrifice if we are to be saved. And now I add two divine appeals, one from the first book of the NT and the other from the last. Matt 11:28: "Come unto me ALL who are weary and heavy burdened", and Rev 22:17: "The Spirit and the bride say 'Come'. And let him that heareth say, 'Come,' and let him that is athirst come. And whosoever will, let him take the water of life freely."

NOTES

1. Foreword to Forster and Marston's book *God's Strategy in Human History*
2. Blaiklock, *Commentary on the N.T.* p.110
3. See Campbell Morgan : *Acts of the Apostles.* p.261

Jacob and Esau
(and associated problem texts)

CAL: There are things in Romans chapter nine which puzzle me, and I should like to begin with verses 11-13, about Jacob and Esau: "For the children being not yet born, neither having done any good or evil, that the purpose of God according to election might stand, not of works, but of Him that calleth; It was said unto her, The elder shall serve the younger. As it is written, Jacob have I loved, but Esau have I hated." Now here, surely, is a statement of absolute election. Here we have the individuals Jacob and Esau with their fate sealed before they were born. Isn't that the case?

JAY: Whose fate was sealed? Paul is talking here about nations, not about individuals.

CAL: But the text says 'children,' not nations - "For the children being not yet born..."

JAY: The words 'the children' are actually not in the original text, and their interpolation obscures Paul's argument. If we go back to Gen 25:23 we find that the Lord said to Rebekah: "Two NATIONS are in thy womb, and two manner of PEOPLES shall be separated from thy bowels; and the one PEOPLE shall be stronger than the other PEOPLE; and the elder shall serve the younger." At this stage you might note that there is no mention of love or hate. I'll refer to that as we go on.

CAL: Augustine applied Romans 9:11 to eternal salvation.

In his *Enchiridion* chapter 25 he took this whole passage of Romans to imply that Esau was damned and Jacob was saved. [1]

JAY. He was wrong in his interpretation, for since the context is that of the two nations Israel and Edom, it would imply that all Edomites were damned and all Israelites were saved. Yet that is the very viewpoint that Paul is attacking in Romans chapter nine! The honoured line of Messiah could not descend through both twins, so God chose what some would call the less promising of the two, in order to magnify His grace (see 1 Cor 1:27-29). Consider the persons: Esau the individual never served Jacob. Indeed it was rather the other way round. It was Jacob who bowed down to Esau, addressing him as 'my lord'. It was Jacob who called himself Esau's servant, begging Esau to accept his gifts. He said that he had seen Esau's face as though he had seen the face of God. Esau certainly did not serve the individual Jacob. It was the nation Esau (Edom) which served the nation Jacob (Israel). Paul's point is that God's choice of Israel was made when both NATIONS were still in the womb, when neither had done either good or evil. The choice of the nation was not a reward for merit, but part of a God-determined strategy. The words of Romans 9:11 refer, not to anyone's eternal destiny, but to the office to which the nation of Israel was elected by God in this life. [2]

CAL: I can follow that explanation, but is not the 'loving' and 'hating' of Jacob and Esau before they were born, like a harsh determinism?

JAY: The Scripture nowhere says that Esau was 'hated' from before he was born. A choice, did take place then. We learn this from the first book of the Bible where it was revealed that one nation would be stronger than the other. Esau was indeed blessed by God through his father Isaac, a lesser blessing than being a Messianic progenitor, it is true. But his destiny is another matter. There is nothing about eternal destiny or 'fates being sealed'. It is not until Malachi, the last book in the Old Testament and over a thousand years later, that we read the words "Esau have I hated."

CAL: That softens the concept - though I should have thought that by that same time Israel also was deserving of such judgement. But please continue...

JAY: Do you think the concept is softened? I'm not so sure, if we read the word 'hate' as in English. As to Israel, she was the elect nation, and Edom incurred the wrath of God because of their unbrotherly conduct towards Israel in the day of Israel's calamity. [3] But although all this is true, the important thing we have to bear in mind is that our English word 'hate' generally does not represent the Hebrew idiom.

CAL: Have we any Scripture for that?

JAY: Yes we do. We get our first indication within the history of Jacob himself. "And he went in also unto Rachel, and he loved also Rachel more than Leah, and served with him yet seven other years. And when the LORD saw that Leah was hated..." (Gen 29:30, 31). The text itself seems to indicate that 'hated' here means 'loved less than'. Barnes says: 'It was common among the Hebrews to use the terms love and hatred in this comparative sense, where the former implied strong positive attachment and the latter, not positive hatred, but merely a less love, or the withholding of expressions of affection.'

The Lord Jesus Himself observes these linguistic conventions of Israel when He says: "If any man come to me, and hate not his father, and mother, and wife, and children...yea, and his own life also, he cannot be my disciple." (Luke 14:26) [4]. Do you think that the Lord Jesus would want us to hate parents and children when He said we were not even to hate our enemies? The parallel text in Matt 10:37 gives the meaning: "He that loveth father and mother *more than me* is not worthy of me: and he that loveth son or daughter *more than me* is not worthy of me." There we see that the word 'hate' is not literal in the sense in which we normally understand it - it implies 'love less than'. (See also Matt 6:24 and Prov 13:24). It means to give priority or preference to one over another.

22

CAL: Can I take it then that when the Bible uses the word 'hate' as a contrast to 'love' it intends us to understand it to mean 'love less than'?

JAY: That seems to be its meaning in all other references, and we must suppose it to be so in Malachi 1:2f. The verse certainly does NOT mean that in a literal hatred of Esau and his descendants God has condemned every one of them to hell. It has reference simply to the higher position of the Hebrew race in the strategy of God. Sanday and Headlam wrote: 'The absolute election of Jacob – the "loving" of Jacob and the "hating" of Esau, has reference simply to the election of one to higher privileges as head of the chosen race, than the other. It has nothing to do with the eternal salvation. In the original to which St. Paul is referring, Esau is simply a synonym for Edom.' [5]

CAL: It's good to learn that.

JAY: Have you more texts for consideration?

CAL: I have a couple of OT texts next: Proverbs 16:4 is one. "The LORD hath made all things for Himself: yea, even the wicked for the day of evil." One commentator (A.W. Pink, I think) has written of that verse: 'It expressly declares that the LORD made the wicked for the day of evil: that was His design in giving them being.' Now I just can't believe that! [6]

JAY: And you are quite right in rejecting that opinion. Let us look at the verse. The AV here once again is misleading. 'For Himself' is not a true rendering. The word means a 'reply' or 'answer'. Indeed it is so translated in verse one: "the answer (or reply) of the tongue..." So then, the phrase might be rendered: "Jehovah has made everything for its purpose." But what does that mean to us? The GNB translates the verse like this: "Everything the LORD has made has its own destiny, and the destiny of the wicked is destruction."

The book of Proverbs has much to say about appropriate

retribution, and in 16:4 says that the wicked person is on his way to his appropriate end. But that does not mean that his destiny is fixed; it doesn't mean that he is hopelessly doomed by an eternal decree. Two verses later, in verse six, we read: "By mercy and truth iniquity is purged: and by the fear of the LORD men depart from evil." The wicked man need not remain wicked. So the LORD urges (Isa 55:7): "Let the wicked forsake his way, and the unrighteous man his thoughts: and let him return unto the LORD, and He will have mercy upon him." Then in Ezekiel 33:11 we read: "I have no pleasure in the death of the wicked; but that the wicked turn from his way and live." [7]

CAL: That clarifies the verse for me. The other OT text is Isa 45:7: "I form the light and create darkness; I make peace, and I create evil: I, the LORD, do all these things." Scofield comments on this verse: "God is not the author of sin (Hab 1:13; 2 Tim 2:13; Titus 1:2; Jas 1:13; Jn 1:5). One of the meanings of the Hebrew word *ra* carries the idea of 'adversity' or 'calamity,' and it is evidently so employed here. God has made sorrow and wretchedness to be the sure fruits of sin." Would you agree with that?

JAY: Yes. God is sovereign, and when He works in human history He can use a Pharaoh, a Sennacherib, a Cyrus, or a Nebuchadnezzar to forward His purposes. Sennacherib boasted of his victories, when he defeated the northern tribes of Israel and transported them. He taunted king Hezekiah with his list of victories as he besieged Jerusalem. But the LORD says, (Isa 37:26): "Hast thou not heard long ago, how I have done it; and of ancient times, that I have formed it? Now have I brought it to pass, that thou shouldest be to lay waste defenced cities into ruinous heaps." Israel had sinned wickedly. Punishment fell upon them, as God had warned them it would if they persisted in their wicked idolatries. He overruled in this, and Assyria was the rod of His anger, though Sennacherib was exercising his own will. Scripture does not detail for us how pagan rulers used their free will in accomplishing God's purposes.

CAL: Thanks for that. But could we turn now to Romans 9:22

please? Here Paul writes - (actually he just poses a question): "What if God, willing to show his wrath, and to make his power known, endured with much longsuffering the vessels of wrath fitted to destruction?" Now here is my difficulty. If the *vessels of wrath* had *been fitted to destruction* by *God's eternal decree*, then how could He be said to endure them with longsuffering if they were just what He made them?

JAY: The verb there can be read as Greek middle voice. So the truth is actually that they 'fitted themselves to destruction'.

CAL: Well, that clears up my difficulty there. But I have some more texts, including Romans 9:18, "Whom He will He hardeneth."

JAY: A consideration of that text would make this discussion far too long. Let's leave it until our next meeting.

NOTES

1. Augustine, *Enchiridion,* chapter 98
2. F. & M. Section 9 (p. 46f)
3. Ps 137:7; Jer 49:7ff; Ezek 25:12ff; Obad 9-19ff; See also Bruce in his *Commentary on Romans*, chap. 9:12
4. F. & M., p. 46
5. F. & M., p. 48 and note no. 15 on p. 49
6. The reference to A W Pink on this page is specifically to p 85 of his book *The Sovereignty of God* (4th edition: Baker House Books, Grand Rapids, 1930).
7. See *Grace Unlimited*, p. 116, article by J A Clines

"Whom He will He hardeneth" (with other problem texts)

CAL: I have great difficulty with that portion in Romans 9 which ends at verse 18: "Therefore hath he mercy on whom he will, and whom he will he hardeneth", and particularly with the thought of hardening. That, and what follows about the potter and the clay, seems to rule out all human responsibility, and to depict God as acting arbitrarily. There is no eluding the force of the words, as far as I can see.

JAY: Let me give you two quotations from others. 'The force of the words is that the mercy and compassion of God cannot be subject to any cause outside His own free grace.' [1] 'The Hebrew phrase used here does not imply any arbitrariness on the part of God, as its English translation might suggest. It simply draws attention to the fact that there are qualities of God which may be seen in certain specific historic instances without going into further detail.' [2]

CAL: I need you to explain that more. Talking about Hebrew phrasing, historic instances and translations into English in this general way, doesn't help my understanding of the principle.

JAY: Remember always *that God desires to have mercy on all.* Paul declares that fact in Romans 11:32. He is not here thinking of those who, like Pharaoh in 9:17, persistently refuse the divine mercy, nor does he intend to make a definite pronouncement about the ultimate destiny of every man. So then, we ask, who are those on whom God will have mercy?

For a brief general answer look at Isaiah 55:7. "Let the wicked forsake his way, and the unrighteous man his thoughts: and let him return unto the LORD, and he will have mercy upon him; and to our God, for he will abundantly pardon." As for those whom He will harden, the Exodus 'historic instance' to which Paul is alluding (Pharaoh, in particular), shows that God hardens those who harden themselves. We shall have to expand on this, but that expresses the truth in a very brief general statement.

CAL: You mean then that the *moral* response of a man – or a nation – is involved?

JAY: Yes, it is. But consider our passage along with Rom 1:26–28, where Paul was declaring a principle on which God always acts: He always gives men up to their own choices. However, don't forget that this Roman letter was written to prove that if these men heard the gospel, and obeyed, they would be saved.

CAL: Doesn't the same principle then hold true in the Old Testament? I have in mind Psalm 81:12 where God says: "So I gave them up unto their own hearts' lust: and they walked in their own counsels."

JAY: Or, as the NIV expresses it: "So I gave them over to their stubborn hearts to follow their own devices." That is a reference to Israel as a nation, and it does illustrate the principle of God's dealing with men and giving them over to their own self-will. But read the next verse, and what follows, and you will see that they were not abandoned. Remember that God in His mercy is always eager to act in grace towards the least glimmer of repentance. Is that clear so far?

CAL: Only partly. Another problem arises in the same context, as I see it. In Ex 20:5 we read: "I the LORD your God am a jealous God, visiting the iniquity of the fathers upon the children unto the third and fourth generation of them that hate me." We have talked about a moral response, but, it seems, there is no possibility of moral responsibility in the case of the poor children here, is there? How are we to understand this?

JAY: The context of verses 4 and 5 is idolatry. Let me quote from a commentary by Campbell Morgan (*This was His Faith* p. 47f). "I think the difficulty (in understanding God to be a 'jealous God') is largely caused by a misunderstanding of the word 'jealous'. The Hebrew word might be rendered with equal accuracy 'zealous'. That is to say, it is a word that marks intensity, even fiery intensity..."

CAL: "The zeal of thine house hath eaten me up." We find these words in John 2:17, quoted from Ps 69:9. Is that the concept?

JAY: Yes. The Greek word used in John 2:17 can mean 'ardour', or 'fervency', in a good sense, and 'jealousy' in a bad sense. But let me continue with my quotation from Campbell Morgan: "It certainly is used to describe that which is evil in some cases. It is equally true that it is used, as in the case of God, to refer to that which has in it NO element such as that of petty vindictiveness, which we now nearly always associate with the word. The declaration that God is a jealous God simply emphasises the irrevocable nature of His laws, and the fact that we cannot escape from them. These laws, I may say, are all the outcome of His love, and are in the interests of men.

"Then, if the passage be read carefully, it will be seen that visiting the iniquities of the fathers upon the children has nothing to do with the GENERAL idea that a child suffers because his father sinned, however true that may be in certain applications, and that it is true all life witnesses. But if you read carefully you will see that the qualifying words are "all of them that hate me". This means that if there is a continuity of hatred of God and disobedience to His laws, there must be continuity of suffering... the whole meaning of the passage is that continuity in rebellion or obedience brings continuity of judgement or reward." Does that long quotation help you?

CAL: Yes... Nevertheless it seems that if the children suffered with the parents, the innocent with the guilty, it was God's doing.

JAY: We shall be considering that more fully. Some commentators make the point that even the visiting "the iniquity of the fathers upon the children unto the third and fourth generation of them that hate me" is far outweighed by "showing mercy (steadfast love, RSV) unto a thousand generations of them that love me". Now, we must ask, how and why was it God's doing? Since God has given man the power to choose (and note that the fundamental laws of the Pentateuch are always addressed to the individual, showing that the responsibility for their observance must always be in the first place individual) [3]; and since this is God's world in which we are all involved with one another, breaches of God's law by one generation *do* affect generations to come. We see that in history, and indeed all around us. We see it where a child is born diseased because of parental immorality. What we usually call 'natural results' are thus an expression of God's law in operation, punishing breaches of His will. We shouldn't blame God if our misdeeds injure others. He made His laws. If we violate them we suffer, and others too may suffer because of our violation. Don't blame God for that. You can't disobey the 'law' of gravity, but if you ignore it, whose fault is it if you break your neck or cause hurt to someone else? Now perhaps you have in mind Scriptures like Deut 24:16: "The fathers shall not be put to death for the children, neither shall the children be put to death for the fathers; every man shall be put to death for his own sin." 2 Kings 14:6 gives us an instance of obedience to this precept, and there are the clear statements of Ezekiel 18. Do you have these in mind?

CAL: Yes, those were Scriptures which I thought of as apparently contradictory. But there is also the episode of Achan and his whole family being put to death for his sin.

JAY: The problem with that episode is not just Achan and his family. Joshua 7:1 says that "*the children of Israel* committed a trespass", and so "the anger of the Lord was kindled against the children of Israel". There was this undoubted solidarity of race and tribe. Evil in the community must be condemned and judged; it can not be condoned. Even in the New Testament we have the idea of the unity of God's community of believers: if one member suffers, the other members suffer with it.

CAL: But isn't that a different context and of different application?

JAY: Maybe. You could look at it that way. But let me continue. The concepts of social solidarity and group responsibility were old in Israel – and human solidarity is an inescapable fact. Ezekiel does not deny that, nor does he deny that corporate suffering affects the righteous also. His words in verses 17 and 20 in their context (and I stress, in their context) do not affirm that the righteous son will not suffer for the sins of his wicked father; they stress that, in the great issues of life, that is, life and death, only the man's own actions are taken into consideration. [4]

CAL: May I say that as you spoke of God "showing mercy unto thousands of them that love me", I thought of the generation that perished in the wilderness and of their children. Though that unbelieving generation died in the wilderness, its sin was not visited upon its children, who indeed entered the Promised Land. Wasn't that a display of God's mercy?

JAY: I think that's a very good example, in the sense that the penalty was not inflicted on the children – for no one would have entered the Promised Land in that case. They did suffer, of course, in having to endure the forty years of wilderness wanderings (Numbers 14:33), because of their parents' 'harlotries'.

CAL: When Ezekiel in chapter 18 quotes the old proverb, "The fathers have eaten sour grapes and the children's teeth are set on edge", he is refuting the whole idea in the proverb, is he not? He is saying that the people must not use such a proverb as an excuse for their own sin.

JAY: Indeed: and although the wicked or thoughtless abuse of man's free will undoubtedly result in many hereditary troubles, there is the spiritual side to be considered. In Ezekiel 18:4 God declares: "Behold, all souls are mine." Let me read to you Campbell Morgan on that declaration. 'The great truth revealed is that every individual has a relationship with God available, which is mightier than all the facts resulting from physical relationships. It may be true that in my physical being I have inherited tendencies to some form of evil from my father, but in the fact of my essential relation to God there are forces available to me more and mightier than all these tendencies. Therefore if I die, it is not because of the sin of my father, but because I fail to avail myself of my resources in God; and if I live, it is because I have availed myself of these resources. Neither righteousness nor evil is hereditary. The former results from right relationship with God and the latter from failure to realise that relationship. All souls are His, and that means that every soul is made for first-hand personal dealing with Him.' Now, before we refer once again to Achan, is that clear so far? [5]

CAL: Yes, I think I now have a better understanding of Ex 20:5. You will be dealing with God's hardening of Pharaoh, so could we for a moment think about Achan? I suppose his family must have been aware of his sin, and so shared it, by not denouncing him. Yet could we really expect a wife and family to have acted otherwise?

JAY: If you read Deut 13:6–11 you may find an answer to that question. The context there is idolatry, but the principle is clear. (We remember that covetousness is idolatry.) No matter how close or intimate the relationship, there must not be any condoning or concealing of the sin. Verse 8 says... "neither shall thine eye pity him, neither shalt thou spare, neither shalt thou conceal him".

CAL: But why was "all that he had" burned too?

JAY: The fact that his inanimate household goods shared in his fate shows that the true explanation is possibly that by bringing the stolen articles into his tent, Achan made it and his family and his goods an extension of Jericho which therefore had to share the fate of Jericho. [6] His sin and its results teach the great truth of the oneness of the people of God: "Israel had sinned". So too, in New Testament terms, the whole cause of Christ is injured by the sin, neglect, or even unspirituality of only one believer. [7] But of course, applications of Scripture must be made rightly. There are those which apply to a soul's salvation and there are those which refer to the disciplining of God's people. They must not be confused.

CAL: Well, things are certainly becoming clearer to me, and I've followed you so far. But I wish you would deal with the 'raising up' of Pharaoh, and with God hardening his heart. I have read that Pharaoh hardened his own heart, but that 'by the ellipses of Hebrew thought, God hardened it, in that He made the laws of mind and heart which Pharaoh violated.' [8] Is that your view?

JAY: There is great truth in that concise statement. Certain laws have been written into our being, and there are inevitable consequences which follow obedience or disobedience of those laws. Where light is rejected, and where righteous obedience is refused, there follows the inevitable hardening of conscience and heart. To us there is a moral problem in the English statement of Romans 9:18. Let us consider it, noting that to the Hebrew writer, there would not be any such problem. He would see God as the First Cause of everything, without in the least minimising the real moral responsibility of the people involved, and without ignoring the means when supernatural activity took place in miracles.

CAL: Could we see that illustrated perhaps in the crossing of the Red Sea? The Israelites could see their miraculous deliverance as due to God's mighty sovereign power, and yet at the same time they could recognise the means employed: God's use of wind and maybe tide? [9]

JAY: Yes, or the raining down of great stones from the sky, later in their history, and so on. There are of course people who try to 'explain away' the miracles of Scripture. They would reject God's supernatural use of His own laws in favour of natural forces acting alone. That would be *their* explanation.

To the believing Hebrew mind, God's action, and His use of the forces of nature in that activity, are one and the same, and having but one explanation. And when it comes to hardening a man's heart, I might add to what I said previously, some words which are frequently quoted in this connection: 'The means by which God hardens a man is not necessarily by any extraordinary intervention on His part; it may be by the ordinary experiences of life, operating through the principles and character of human nature, which are of His appointment.' [10]

CAL: This statement of Scripture – which still puzzles me – where God says of Pharaoh, 'For this cause have I raised thee up', can be translated as 'I have caused thee to stand'. Isn't that right?

JAY: It is. And the Septuagint means: 'thou wast preserved'. The reference may be, not merely to God's raising up Pharaoh to be king, but to His patience in preserving him alive. [11] We may notice also as we study this, that Pharaoh was not alone in the 'hardening' process; his servants were in it too. Now observe that God gave clear warning to Pharaoh in Ex 9:18 of the grievous hail, and instruction in the following verse about ensuring the safety of man and beast. What happened? Those of Pharaoh's servants that 'feared the word of the LORD' saved their slaves and cattle, and those who 'regarded not the word of the LORD' took no action, and so suffered loss.

CAL: So then, would you say that Pharaoh and his servants could have repented at an early stage?

JAY: Yes. They could have yielded. The plagues gradually increased in severity and they were always solemnly announced.

CAL: Yet how could this happen when God definitely said He would cause Pharaoh to stand – or to harden his heart? That is my difficulty. There was a definite pronouncement of judgement.

JAY: You are raising an important issue which is indeed a problem for some people as they read through the prophetic pronouncements of judgement. We must beware of having any fatalistic notions concerning the prophecies. Take the case of Nineveh in the book of Jonah. Nothing could have been more definite or explicit than Jonah's pronouncement that in forty days Nineveh would be destroyed. Yet it was not destroyed. Why not? Had the prophecy failed? If we consider Jeremiah 18:7-10 and 26:3, 13 we may find the answer. Let's look at those verses now, please.

CAL: I have the NIV here. It reads: *"If at any time I announce that a nation or kingdom is to be uprooted, torn down and destroyed, and if that nation I warned repents of its evil, then I will relent and not inflict on it the disaster I had planned. And if at another time I announce that a nation or kingdom is to be built up and planted, and if it does evil in my sight and does not obey me, then I will reconsider the good I had intended to do for it."* Chapter 26 verse 3 reads: "Perhaps they will listen and each will turn from his evil way. Then I will relent and not bring on them the disaster I was planning because of the evil they have done." Verse 13 reads: "Now reform your ways and your actions and obey the LORD your God. Then the LORD will relent and will not bring the disaster he has pronounced against you." Could we assume from those Scriptures that the predictions of judgement in the Old Testament prophecies are conditional upon no repentance, even if the condition is not expressly stated?

JAY: I believe that to be so. There was no expressed condition in Jonah's prophecy: it was terrible in its stark unconditional brevity. The people of Nineveh however acted in the hope that by repenting and turning from their evil ways, they would avert the prophesied doom. And so they did; their hope was justified. And it is obvious from Jonah's attitude that he knew this could happen, as we read in chapter 4:2 : "O LORD, is this not what I said when I was still at home? That is why I was so quick to flee to Tarshish. I knew that you are a gracious and compassionate God, slow to anger and abounding in love, a God who relents from sending calamity." (NIV) So, even where there is a definite pronouncement of judgement, it may not descend if repentance takes place. That does not mean that the prophecy has failed. There will be no need for the threatened doom or punishment where the prophecy results in humbling and obedience. That illustration of Nineveh is very important as bearing on God's mercy and grace, and I trust that its relevance is clear to you. [12]

CAL: I do see its relevance, yet, as God said to Pharaoh: "For this cause have I raised thee up, for to shew in thee my power" (Ex 9:16). How could God's power have been seen if Pharaoh had given in?

JAY: You must keep in mind God's purposes. He could have shown His power by killing all the Egyptians at the very beginning and so leaving Israel to go out unhindered. (Cf. Exodus 9:15, NIV.)

CAL: What then was His fuller purpose in dealing with Pharaoh?

JAY: Let's recapitulate a bit. You have quoted from Exodus 9 where the seventh blow is about to fall. Pharaoh is warned of impending judgement so that he may acknowledge not only God's power, but also recognise the uniqueness of the God of Israel. As we read the passage, we realize that hitherto the plagues came in mercy rather than in penal judgement, for each one was an opportunity for Pharaoh to repent. I think Moffatt puts the whole situation very clearly. Listen to his translation, beginning at verse 13, with my emphases: "The Eternal said to Moses, Appear before the Pharaoh early in the morning, and tell him this from the Eternal, the God of the Hebrews: 'Let my people go, to worship me. For this time I will rain all these my strokes on you and your officers and your people *to teach you that there is no one like me in all the world.* Otherwise, I would have exerted my force and struck you and your people with pestilence till you were swept off the earth, but *this is why I have kept you alive*, to let YOU see my power and to publish my fame all over the world.'" Now comes verse 17. In the AV it comes in the form of a question: "As yet exaltest thou thyself against my people, that thou wilt not let them go?" The idea behind the 'exalting' himself is 'being obstructionist.' Moffatt again clearly expresses the thought: "You still thwart my people, refusing to let them go?" There then follows the warning of the terrible hail. The NIV translates the verse, not as a question, but as a statement with a following 'therefore'. "You still set yourself against my people and will not let them go, therefore..." The judgement will descend, but with the given opportunity to save livestock and people from the hail.

CAL: Pharaoh's responsibility in all that seems to be clear.

JAY: I agree. Now then, as to God's purposes, we might set them out something like this: firstly, to redeem Israel from Egypt, with everything that is involved in their becoming the nation of God's chosen people (Ex 6:6-7), that they should clearly understand who had delivered them, and that they should hand down this knowledge to their children (Ex 10:2; 13:1-15).

Secondly, that they should not go away empty, but carry possessions with them from Egypt. Thirdly, that God might multiply His signs and bring His people forth in great acts, so that both Pharaoh and the Egyptians themselves should know that He was the true God, the only God. Why? Because the Egyptians, like other nations at that time, were idolaters. Their gods 'were numerous indeed, supposedly inhabiting the heavens, the earth and the subterranean regions. It would be impossible to bring judgement in any one of these three spheres without touching one or more deities of Egypt. The ten plagues were designed as visitations on the Egyptians and their gods at the same time. Thus, the plague of darkness was directed against the sun-god Ra, the most prominent of the Egyptian deities' (Scofield note on Ex 8:2 - and see Ex 12:2). See also Num 33:4.

CAL: I never thought of it like that, but it occurs to me now that Egypt's great serpent emblem was shown to be defeated too – in Ex 7:12 – right at the start of the contest.

JAY: That's true. But finally (I was about to say) God's purpose was that His name might be declared not only in Egypt but in the whole earth. [13]

CAL: I suppose if Israel had been faithful then this would have been so, and He would have been recognised throughout the world as the only true God. Centuries later the Philistine priests and diviners could say to their lords and people: "Why then do you harden your hearts as the Egyptians and Pharaoh hardened their hearts? When he had wrought wonderfully among them, did they not let the people go? and they departed?" They urged that glory should be given to the God of Israel, but to them He was just another local god. (1 Sam 6:6)

JAY: Alas for the failures of the people of God! It is interesting to note however that Pharaoh's attitude was remembered even in Philistia. Now let me refer to your earlier question about Pharaoh 'giving in'. There are two ways in which he could have done so: by repentance, or in sheer fear.

CAL: Surely God would rather have had Pharaoh repent than perish in the Red Sea?

JAY: Assuredly: and we can never know what blessing God would have wrought had Pharaoh and the Egyptians truly repented. Our limited vision of God's possible actions does not alter the truth of that. Do remember also that in this Exodus story to which Paul makes reference, what is at stake is not the eternal destiny of an individual soul. God is working out His strategy through the nation of Israel.

CAL: Before we close this part of our discussion, my understanding of our subject is as follows. The overall effect of God's actions was that Pharaoh was confirmed in his obduracy. The LORD knew Pharaoh and his character, and knew what his reactions would be to Moses' request. The LORD knew that the way His power would be revealed, little by little as the plagues progressed, would have the effect of stimulating Pharaoh into obduracy. God was responsible for this process (in sending the plagues of progressively more obvious origin). But Pharaoh was also responsible – in his unrepentant reaction to these.

JAY: Yes, but I would like to add to that a quote on the Hebrew of Exodus by Kalisch: 'As the external, often accidental *occasion* of an event is mostly more obvious, even to the reflecting mind, than its primary cause or its true (often hidden) originator, it has become a linguistic peculiarity in most ancient, especially the Semitic, languages, to use indiscriminately the former instead of the latter, so that the phrase "I shall harden the heart of Pharaoh" means "I know that I shall be *the cause* of Pharaoh's obstinacy: my commandments and wonders will be an *occasion,* an *inducement* to an increasing obduration of his heart." And the compassionate leniency of God, who, instead of crushing the refractory king with one powerful blow, first tried to reform him by various less awful punishments, and who generally announced the time of the occurrence of the plagues by the words: "Behold, I shall afflict tomorrow", in order to grant him time for reflection and repentance; this clemency on the part of God increased Pharaoh's refractoriness; it was to him a cause of prolonged and renewed resistance.' [14]

CAL: I find that quotation helps me to understand a lot better. I conclude that Pharaoh was no mere automaton, no helpless puppet.

JAY: I agree. There is very much more which we could consider in this area, but I suggest that you read the more extensive study on which I have based so many of my answers. [15]

CAL: I'll do that. Perhaps in our next discussion we could move on to the 'potter and the clay' texts which seem so fatalistic to me.

NOTES

1. Bruce, Romans 9:15 (p. 192). It is God's desire to have mercy on all.
2. See Cole on Ex. 33:19.
3. See Ellison. chap. 8 (p. 72).
4. See Ellison. chap. 8 (p. 73).
5. Campbell Morgan. *Searchlights from the Word,* p. 262f.
6 See Ellison. chap.8 (p.71). And see Joshua 5:17, 18 for strong warnings.
7. 1 Cor. 5:1-7; 12: 14-26
8. Blaiklock. *Commentary on the New Testament,* on Romans 9:1-29
9. If we were to agree with Velikovsky's *Worlds in Collision,* we would see more than winds and tides involved .

10. Cole (quoting Driver) on Exodus (p.77f).
11. Bruce on Romans 9:17 (p.194).
12. See Bruce 'A. to Q.', p. 129f. for fuller treatment of this.
13. See F.& M. (p. 59f). and Scofield's note on Ex. 8:2.
14. F. & M., p. 131.
15. See F. & M. on these issues, especially the 'Word Study, 'Harden.' p.125 et seq.

The Potter and the Clay

JAY: If we look at Paul's quotation in Romans 9:21 without considering the background of Isaiah and Jeremiah then his words may indeed present a rather fatalistic image. They would not have done so to Paul's Hebrew opponent, who would have known the Old Testament background of the parable of the potter in Jeremiah chapter 18. Let us turn to Jeremiah first. What did he see?

CAL: He watched the potter at work, and verse four says: "And the vessel that he made of clay was marred in the hand of the potter: so he made it again another vessel, as seemed good to the potter to make it."

JAY: Notice that he refashioned it. The vessel was not destroyed. Then follows the word of the LORD: "O house of Israel, cannot I do with you as this potter? saith the LORD."

CAL: Refashioned or not, surely that word of the LORD means that Israel had no active part in the finished vessel. Israel is just like clay being moulded by a potter and, in the next chapter, we do have the image of a vessel being destroyed in the sight of the elders or rulers.

JAY: Let us examine this. In chapter 18 verses 4 to 6, God demonstrates to Jeremiah that He is able to take the marred vessel Israel, and make it anew into a vessel of usefulness, but to the elders in chapter 19 the prophet has to declare that their generation will be destroyed like a broken clay vessel, and the fragments taken to Babylon. Now, read what comes in between those two episodes.

CAL: Immediately following the LORD's message to them that they are in His hands as clay in the hands of the potter, there comes the Scripture which we have already considered, about God's principle in dealing with a nation - He will not pluck up, pull down or destroy it if it repents; He will not build up or plant it if it becomes disobedient and turns to evil.

JAY . The lesson there is as we saw before, that the LORD will deal with a nation according to its own moral response. That robs the potter and the clay image of any immoral fatalism. Remember that *'A mechanical determinism annihilates morality.'* [1]

CAL: Chapter 18 verse 11 would seem to bear out what you say. There the prophet is instructed to appeal to the men of Judah. They are warned of judgement, and are urged individually to repent – that is, to turn from their evil ways, and to do good. In the next verse they refuse to do so, and indeed there follows great opposition against Jeremiah, the prophet of the LORD. So the chapter 19 episode of the broken pot would seem to indicate that, accordingly, judgement must follow.

JAY: The lesson there is clear and, although I have emphasised that there is no place for fatalism in it, there are two factors to be kept in view. The first, which we have just observed, is that obedience or disobedience to the will of God determines whether or not a nation will be built up and established or broken down; whether it becomes a vessel unto honour or dishonour. The second is that God alone decides how the finished vessels or the resulting work will fit into His plan. The overall strategy is His.

CAL: Yes, I see that now. And so far as the image of the shattered pot is concerned, if we think of individual souls and salvation, it does not imply that God ever looks on men as things to be shattered, since He loves His creatures and He would have all men to come to a knowledge of the truth. Would you agree with that?

JAY: Yes. God suffered in Christ for men. He does not think of them as insentient and irresponsible clay. [2]

CAL: Yet Paul's statements in this portion have often been read to mean that a man must not question God's ways, and indeed to mean that God's will for the individual is irresistible. Surely that view is not correct?

JAY: It is not, for that was not Paul's view. Men are not clay pots. They were made in the image of God, and so they will raise questions. But why, and how, they do so, is important. Moses, Job, Jeremiah, the Psalmist, Habakkuk and others brought their anguished questions to strong utterance. And even from the Christ on the Cross there came that cry of a profound sense of dereliction, "My God, why hast Thou forsaken me?" Bruce comments, 'When the man of faith cries out like this it is precisely because the righteousness of God, as well as His power, is the major premiss of all his thinking.' The tragic facts of life may rise in seeming fearsome contradiction of God's holiness and justice, and His servants will cry out, 'Why?' God does not condemn the sincere questioner. 'God, in His grace, does abide His people's question; but He will not be cross-examined at the judgement bar of a hard and impenitent heart.' [3]

CAL: I can follow that. But does God always answer? Are not His servants often left in the dark, so to speak?

JAY: Your question goes away beyond our enquiry, and takes us into the wide-ranging area of prayer. We are here concerned with whether or not God permits any questioning of His ways, and I think we agree that He does. But I cannot leave your question unanswered, so here is a very brief reply, because God always answers, though in different ways. It is His will in His training of us for His purposes in government – His training of our characters for eternity – that in this life we walk by faith and not by sight. "Blessed are they who have not seen, and yet have believed," was our Lord's word to His erstwhile doubting disciple (John 20:29). I do not mean that God always gives a straightforward, or direct, answer to our questionings, nor that His answer will be an intellectual solution to the problem we raise before Him. It is rather that He reveals more of Himself to us in our searching. He draws out our faith and trust in Himself, sometimes revealing enough of His purposes where that is necessary to strengthen the faith of His beleaguered servants. Paul quoted Habakkuk: "The just shall live by his faith", and a study of Habakkuk would be rewarding for you. I here simply ask you to notice that he did not arrive at a new-found faith because of a vision of green pastures and quiet waters. His final confidence and tranquillity was the attainment of a renewed appreciation of the LORD in whom he trusted, a faith in the LORD exercised in the face of impending calamity: national economic ruin and famine, we might say. In our own lives we may recall circumstances which were undesirable and hard to explain, but which led to a new and deeper understanding of the accepted truth, "The LORD is my refuge". I will say no more on this now. I recommend you to study the prayers of Moses, Hannah, the people in the wilderness lusting for flesh, Paul's prayers for the removal of the thorn in his flesh, and the answers given to those prayers. [4]

CAL: I do not want to deflect our discussion further, but there is one other thing which troubles me. The question, "Why hast Thou made me thus?" often comes before me when I see people who have been physically or mentally handicapped from birth. I wonder why this is, but I would not wonder if *they* were to cry, "Why hast Thou made me thus?" This is not our subject, but I should value your comments.

JAY: I have no answer at all to the problem posed by your question, and I think it's unwise to proffer the glib answers sometimes given by others to people in tragic circumstances, well-meant though the words may be. But I will say this: what strikes me with wonder is how so many afflicted people do *not* rise up in bitter questioning. I am surprised at the way they often react: the unvarying cheerfulness of some blind people I have known; the mouth and foot painting artists who achieve such a triumph of the human spirit over their severe handicaps; the heroic efforts of the physically handicapped in the 'Paraplegics Olympics'; the uncomplaining burden-bearing of many who endure things under which I should sink. These both reproach and inspire me. We who possess healthy bodies and minds – how comparatively little some of us achieve, and how little makes us complain! I am convinced that the sufferings caused by the tragedies of life are not God's will for us, but I should not attempt any explanation such as original sin, chastening, or the abuse of man's freewill. I put forward no answer. There is however one thing certain: the disease and distress around us, the trials and tragedy in the lives of others, should move us out of selfish concern for our own well-being into greater compassion and concern for others. When God blesses us, He does so in order that we may be a blessing to others. I do not construe the story of the rich man and Lazarus in Luke 16 as suggesting a balanced future in eternity. I see no warrant for that in Scripture. But to the question, "Shall not the Judge of all the earth do right?" there must be given a cosmic affirmative. As this is not our subject, I say no more on it; I am aware of the inadequacy of my words.

CAL: Thank you. But I have led you away from our text, and we must return to it. Paul's imaginary critic is a Hebrew, yet he asks, "Why does He yet find fault, for who withstands His will?" Since the critic would know the Old Testament and would be aware that God's will had indeed been resisted in the past, why does he raise such a question?

JAY: Let us not say that the critic is merely a creation of Paul's imagination; he must have met him often enough in past controversies. He, like Paul, would accept the doctrines of the Old Testament as authoritative, but he would not accept all Paul's applications of them. In this context the critic may be objecting to the way in which, according to Paul, God was using his nation without any reference to the merits which he supposed Israel to possess. So he resists Paul's revelation of God's ways. It was this sort of situation in Israel's past which we see in Isaiah, and which we must now consider.

It has been expressed as follows: 'The prophet Isaiah had a similar vision of God using some specially chosen figure in the shaping of Israel's history. Cyrus, a heathen king, was anointed as God's shepherd for the sake of God's chosen servant (people)

Israel. At that time, just as in the time of Paul, someone objected to God controlling such temporal features of His creation and using His anointed Cyrus and servant Jacob in these ways. Isaiah attacked such people who thought themselves wiser than God. "Woe unto him that strives with his Maker...shall the clay say to Him that fashions it, what are you making? Or your work, he has no hands? (handles)" (45:9). As we saw in Jeremiah 18, the lesson of the potter deciding how the vessel would fit into his plans, so here. Special privileges, such as the election of a nation to further God's purposes are decided by Him, for He alone knows the best strategy to fulfil His plans. It would be ridiculous for a mere creature to set itself up as knowing better. Notice, however, that Isaiah there, like Paul in Romans 9, was concerned with God's movements in history and not with the final destiny of the individuals involved.' [5]

CAL: I don't think I need further clarification on that. There are other Scriptures which I still need to examine with you, but those Scriptures which we have had before us dispose of any fatalistic theory, by God's frequent appeals to men to repent and obey. "Why will ye die?" He says through Jeremiah (27:13). In Luke 7:30 we see that the Pharisees and experts in the Law rejected God's purposes for themselves; and, just before his death, Stephen charged the Sanhedrin with always resisting the Holy Spirit. The truth seems to be then, that although nothing can thwart God's ultimate purposes, yet men can, and do, rebel against God's will for themselves.

JAY: That is the sad fact. Campbell Morgan once wrote a letter in which he said: 'I remember always that God created man in His own image and likeness, which means, among other things, having the magnificent and yet awe-inspiring power and freedom of the will. Man has used that will in rebellion, and ... suffering and wrong is the result of man's action. I say it with profound reverence that God, by the very nature of the case, cannot prevent these things, but He is overruling them. Man is being compelled under the pressure of the Divine government to work out his own choices. It is equally certain that the ultimate victory will be with the righteousness and mercy of God.' [6]

CAL: I was thinking, as you spoke of the 'magnificent yet awe-inspiring power and freedom of the will', of Rev.3:20. "Behold, I stand at the door, and knock; if any man hear my voice, and open the door...I will come in to him..." The Lord will not force the door; but where there is the least willingness, then He will come in both to will and to work with us. It seems incredible, but it is His own very word.

JAY: That's a wonderful truth! How sad it is when such willingness is absent. We hear that sadness in the Saviour's lament over Jerusalem: "O Jerusalem, Jerusalem, thou that killest the prophets, and stonest them who are sent unto thee, how often would I have gathered thy children together, even as a hen gathereth her chickens under her wings, and ye would not!" (Matt. 23:37). The responsibility was theirs, and the Saviour was grieved at His rejection by them.

CAL: The thought of that Jewish unbelief troubles me, for some of the texts seem to indicate that they had no say in their unbelief, and yet I know that can't be true. Could we discuss that at our next meeting please?

JAY: We'll do that if you wish, but I warn you that there are no easy answers.

NOTES

1. Dodd on Rom. 9:19 (p. 171 of *Commentary on Romans*).
2. Blaiklock. *Commentary on the New Testament* Chap. 9 (p. 135). See also F.& M. p. 64ff on this.
3. See Bruce on Romans 9 (p. 189f).
4. God may answer 'Yes', 'No', or 'Not yet'. See Ex 5:22, 23 and God's answer to Moses in chapter six; see 1 Sam. 1:10, 11. Hannah's first son was to be a man of destiny in God's purposes for Israel. She had to wait God's timing, and to be prepared to co-operate in those purposes. See Ps 106:12-15 for a request granted – but with what results! See 2 Cor 12:7-9 for the Apostle Paul's

response to God's denial of his oft repeated earnest request. See *The Silence of God* by Sir Robert Anderson, p. 203 et seq on 'The Value of Prayer'.

5. F. & M. p. 64.

6. Campbell Morgan, *This Was His Faith* p. 212.

Jewish Unbelief

CAL: I still have difficulty with some texts concerning Israel's blindness. Perhaps you could explain them for me, even if that means going over ground which we have already covered. There is the bald statement in Mark 4:12 that "seeing they may see, and not perceive, and hearing they may hear, and not understand; lest at any time they should be converted, and their sins should be forgiven them." John 12:39 is even stronger: "Therefore they could not believe, because that Isaiah said again, He hath blinded their eyes", and so on. "Therefore they could not believe" is the phrase I find hard to explain. Then in John 6:44 Jesus said, "No man can come to me, except the Father who hath sent me draw him." Yet in 5:40 He charges the Jews in the words: "And ye will not come to me, that ye might have life." There are two other texts ...

JAY: Let's look first at those you have mentioned.

CAL: Yes, but let me say something first by way of prelude. I realise that there can be no contradiction in our Lord's sayings, yet there are many which I do not understand, especially in John's gospel. It seems to me that our Lord at times intentionally obscured His meaning; that He was enigmatic on occasions, even when He was asked a direct question. He used parables in the first three gospel records, but not in John's record of His ministry. Does John indicate that Jesus did deliberately veil His teaching at times?

JAY: The short answer to your question must be that there were indeed occasions when Jesus did not respond as His questioners desired. They were not ready for that. He had to disguise or veil His deeper meanings at times. If we agree that He did so, then we have to ask some questions. What was it which was hidden or disguised? From whom was it veiled, and for what reason? You mentioned parables, as though the Lord in the first three gospel records taught plainly at all times, whilst His teaching in John's record was obscured or enigmatic. Why do you think our Lord used parables at all?

CAL: I was taught that He used them simply to illustrate His teaching, to make His meaning plain. That is why Mark 4:12 and associated texts in the other gospels puzzle me.

JAY: There are many misconceptions about the parables of the Lord Jesus. He did use allegories and illustrations in all the Gospel records. But so far as the parables of the kingdom are concerned, there is even now no agreement as to their full interpretation. Commentators differ widely, and it is not our purpose to examine those differing interpretations. Our Lord Himself was asked why He used parables, so let us hear His own answer. We have the fullest account of His words in Matthew chapter 13. Read verses 10 to 17, please.

CAL: These read (NIV): "The disciples came to him and asked, 'Why do you speak to the people in parables?' He replied, 'The knowledge of the secrets of the kingdom of heaven has been given to you, but not to them. Whoever has will be given more, and he will have an abundance. Whoever does not have, even what he has will be taken from him. This is why I speak to them in parables. Though seeing they do not see; though hearing, they do not hear or understand. In them is fulfilled the prophecy of Isaiah: You will be ever hearing but never understanding; you will be ever seeing but never perceiving. For this people's heart has become calloused; they hardly hear with their ears, and they have closed their eyes. Otherwise they might see with their eyes, hear with their ears, understand with their hearts and turn, and I would heal them. But blessed are your eyes because they see, and your ears because they hear. For I tell you the truth, many prophets and righteous men longed to see what you see but did not see it, and to hear what you hear but did not hear it.'" That's down to verse 17. According to that passage, the teaching of Jesus was veiled from some.

JAY: It was. Notice first, that parables are not always understood without explanation, though they are meant to teach a lesson – to bring home with force the truth presented. David did not understand Nathan's parable of the man and the ewe lamb until the prophet declared: "Thou art the man!" (2 Sam. 12:7). The force of the truth in the parable then shocked him. Our Lord's enigmatic sayings in John's gospel and His parabolic teaching about the kingdom (the revelation of the mysteries of the kingdom in parables) was due to the existence of two distinct groups in Israel at that time; two groups which had become polarised by then. Let us look at them.

All these men among whom the ministry of the Lord Jesus had been exercised had preliminary knowledge of the ways of God as a result of the religion in which they had been born and trained. Jesus was not among pagan Gentiles. He had come "unto His own". In fulfilment of their own Scriptures, He had come. Certain of them received Him, and others of them had rejected Him. We have these two groups: the latter group seeking to establish their own righteousness without regard to faith or the mind of God on the question; the other group containing those who had received John's baptism of repentance and who in faith were waiting for God to reveal His coming kingdom: one group hardening into rejectors, and one group drawn to the Lord Jesus. All the Jews were given God's teaching, but only those who listened to God, and heard from Him, were drawn to the Lord Jesus. The disciples were in the category of those who had responded in faith to Him, and their loyalty was to Him. They already possessed some truth regarding Messiah and His programme. Their understanding of that was not great, but careful reflection on the parables would enlighten them further. "Whosoever hath, to him shall be given, and he shall have in abundance." They were in that category. The other group, those determined unbelievers who had refused the previous teaching of Jesus (chapters ten and eleven) were not being given the plain bare truths to "trample underfoot". Yet there is grace even here, some would tell us, for they were spared the greater guilt of rejecting the plainer teaching. There did remain the possibility for them that the intriguing parable would arouse their curiosity and interest, and so lead to repentance and a change of heart. That is God's desire for all men. Nevertheless, if they failed to repent, they were in danger of losing what they already had, the real value of all they had gained through their early religious nurture and training. "To him that hath not, from him shall be taken even that which he hath." That was their category. [1] Have you followed me so far?

CAL: That does help, but I am still not clear about it all. If we look at the end of our Lord's answer in that portion, we read that many righteous men and prophets desired to see those things but did not live to see them. Yet those men were obviously right with God.

JAY: And it is equally obvious, our Lord was not concealing the way to a right relationship with God. He was not hiding from any of His hearers something which would enable them to go to heaven instead of hell. The *need for repentance* was not concealed.

CAL: Well, yes, I see that. What was hidden involves "the mysteries of the kingdom of heaven", but how should we understand those words?

JAY: That's not really our subject, but I'll answer you as briefly as I can. We read in Matt. 13:35 that this peculiar approach via parables was linked to an OT prophecy: "That it might be fulfilled which was spoken by the prophet, saying. I will open my mouth in parables; I will utter things which have been kept secret from the foundation of the world." In passing, note that the Greek word here rendered 'parable' is the Septuagint translation of the Hebrew word *mashal* which denotes 'a difficult or enigmatic saying'. That would corroborate the opinion that the parables of the kingdom in Matt. 13 are not just simple illustrations. [2]

Now, the glories of the Messianic reign were clearly delineated in the Old Testament, but the rejection of Messiah, and the interval between His first and second comings, were not understood. These parables are meant to bring home to Israel the fuller truth of the prophecies of Scripture. Israel was God's vineyard: the field is the world. There is a difference between labouring only in the vineyard and "Go ye out into all the world." That difference must now be taught, because of the nation's rejection of the Lord. It has been said that the parables describe the strange form of the kingdom during the absence of the King. They are about what God is doing in history, and what He will do in the last times. A period of time had to elapse between Messiah's suffering and His glory, and the mysteries of the kingdom relate to that interval.

CAL: I can follow what you say, but I am not satisfied that you have answered the 'why' concerning the 'veiling' of the teaching, since the disciples themselves didn't understand the parables any more than the other listeners; they had to ask for an explanation. Am I being obtuse?

JAY: Not at all; I appreciate your difficulty. For a fuller understanding of our Lord's motives in that parabolic teaching, I think we must study His statement about giving what is holy unto the dogs, and casting pearls before swine (Matt. 7:6).

CAL: I always thought that was a terribly strong expression: dogs and swine. The Gentiles were sometimes called *dogs* by the Jews. Is that fact relevant here?

JAY: I don't think so. It was primarily an admonitory proverbial expression. The statement of it comes after our Lord's warning about censorious judgement. Campbell Morgan writes on this: 'Then there is a sudden change. "Give not that which is holy unto the dogs, neither cast your pearls before swine, lest they trample them under their feet, and turn again and rend you." We are not to be critically censorious, but we must exercise discrimination and discretion. There are characters we must discern and be careful of, for there are things committed to our care which we must safeguard at all costs. This may appear a rough description of the characters, but the King makes use of no vulgar descriptions save when He is describing vulgar things. Who are 'the dogs', 'the swine'? Let Scripture interpret Scripture. No doubt Peter heard Him say this, and after he had passed through very wonderful experiences he wrote, and used words his Master used. "It has happened to them according to the true proverb, The dog turning to his own vomit again, and the sow that had washed to her wallowing in the mire." (2 Pet. 2:22). "It has happened unto them..." In the previous chapter we have a remarkable exposition of these words of Jesus. The chapter begins with false prophets. As we go on through the chapter we have the terrible teaching that, though we may be in the place of privilege and blessing, if we turn our back upon it we must be cast out therefrom. It is a terrible and dark description of certain men who resolutely set themselves against holy things, but who come into holy places to traffic with holy things with unholy purposes – dogs, who presently will go back to their vomit; swine, who presently will be back to their wallowing in the mire.' [3] I end the quote there. Now let us think of the words which Jesus uttered. They applied particularly to His situation in view of the reaction of some of the Jews to the miracle of healing (John 5:16). They completely ignored the healing and sought to slay Jesus. What do you think would have happened had He at that time openly proclaimed Himself to be Messiah and the chief Heir to the kingdom of Heaven?

CAL: Would that not have led to His immediate arrest and trial?

JAY: I have no doubt about that. I think we may fairly say that to avoid that happening before His "His hour had come", the Lord disguised from His enemies and the unspiritual the truth (the pearls) which He taught, and so kept them uncertain of His meaning. There would have been no uncertainty had they accepted Him in His true character, of course.

CAL: We see the uncertainty in chapter 10 verse 19 where there was a division of the Jews over His words.

JAY: We do. And just after that, verse 24, they put to Him the blunt question: "If thou be the Christ, tell us plainly." His answer was indirect. It had to be so. Their misconception of the work of Messiah blinded them to the *true* Messianic work. They cherished the idea of military conquest - victory over the Romans - and political rule, with a temporal king on a royal throne. For Jesus at that stage to have said He was Messiah (the anointed King) would have been to confirm their erroneous thought of Him: to have said He was not would have been to contradict the essential truth. He referred them, then, to His earlier words and deeds in proof of who He is. Far from victory over the Romans and a royal throne awaiting Him, He faced suffering and a violent death. Even His disciples, who had been instructed not to tell anyone that He was the Messiah, could not take that in. So, His reply to those questioning people, was intentionally equivocal, but in it He nevertheless implied that those who were right with God would understand His meaning. To the genuine seeker after truth, Jesus would explain as required. We learn from Mark 4:10–12 that there were others beside the Twelve who questioned Him about the parables *and who were answered.* To those who tried to trap Him, however, and to the uninterested, the principle of Matt 7:6 would apply: pearls are not for trampling underfoot by the unappreciative and foes; pearls are not for pigs; the unholy are not to be given that which is holy.

CAL: Can we say then that the Lord's *interested* listeners learned the meaning of the truth which He taught from God the Father (John 6:45) while His *enemies* who heard the same teaching did not understand it?

JAY: We can indeed. The Lord's opponents had the Scriptures. They studied them, and some of them taught the Scriptures. Yet Jesus had to say to them that they did not have God's word abiding in them, nor had they the love of God in them (John 5:38, 42). They didn't even believe Moses, and so were to be blamed. Who would accuse them? Not the Lord, but Moses, whom they professed to trust. So, because they did not believe their own Scriptures – which pointed to Messiah – they could not believe the words of Jesus (John 5:45–47). Had they believed the Word of God, the Father would have drawn them to the Son. Let us note here that the *initiative* in drawing men is with God the Father, but men may *resist* that drawing. So Jesus justifiably charges them in the words: "Ye will not come to me that ye might have life."

From these references we learn two important facts. Firstly, the reason for Jewish unbelief was that the Jews closed their own eyes in case the truth were uncomfortable for them: they didn't want that sort of spiritual kingdom with its moral demands and implications. Secondly, the Lord was enigmatic on occasions and taught in parables so that the spiritual among His hearers would be stimulated from right motives to enquire His meaning, while the real treasure of the truth that He taught would be concealed from His enemies and from the uninterested. Is that sufficiently clear?

CAL: Much more than before. Nevertheless there are still Scripture texts for which I can see no explanation. The first is John 12:39-40, where we have the definite statement: "Therefore they could not believe, because that Isaiah said again, He hath blinded their eyes, and hardened their heart..." etc.

JAY: Let us discuss that text first, though you are really asking me to retread ground already covered. However, put the text in context. Read verses 37 to 43, please.

CAL: It reads: "But though He had done so many miracles before them, yet they believed not on Him: That the saying of Isaiah the prophet might be fulfilled, which he spoke, Lord, who hath believed our report? ...Therefore they could not believe, because that Isaiah said again, He hath blinded their eyes, and hardened their heart: that they should not see with their eyes, nor understand with their heart, and be converted, and I should heal them. These things said Isaiah, when he saw His glory, and spoke of Him. Nevertheless among the chief rulers also many believed on Him, but because of the Pharisees they did not confess Him, lest they should be put out of the synagogue: For they loved the praise of men more than the praise of God."

JAY: Thank you. That is a summary of the ministry of Jesus as

John saw it. Now of course, and quite clearly, the purpose of this final summary of the ministry of Jesus is not meant to deny the whole purpose of John's own record, of his Gospel, as though it was impossible for the Jews to recognise Jesus as the Son of God. It is to point out that the rejection of the Messiah by His own people ought not to surprise those familiar with the Old Testament Scriptures (cf. Hoskyns/Tasker: note 2). We are certainly not to understand that their unbelief was the result of direct divine action. God does not take that sort of action. He does ratify human decision, as we saw earlier in connection with Pharaoh, and with the potter and the clay. If, in spite of all the signs, men refuse the evidence of the signs, there comes the hour when the choice is ratified by God and they pass into the realm of blindness.

CAL: Could we call that a judicial penalty? A judicial hardening?

JAY: If the terms are rightly understood, yes. I dislike such terms however, as they often have different meanings for different people. If you mean that God has so made us that refusal to heed the Word of God results in a calloused state, a state of moral insensitiveness, I would agree. Unbelief is sin, and Temple has given this comment: 'God does not cause sin, but He does cause its appropriate consequence to result from it by the law of the order of creation.' [4] John is here (chap. 12), referring to Isaiah chapter six. The Scripture he cites is quoted in two other places in the New Testament at what we might call crucial turning points: in Matthew 13 it is quoted at the point where Jesus changed from teaching openly to using parables, as we saw earlier. It was a time when, it seems, He turned away from the nation as a whole to teach only those who were spiritually discerning. The other great turning point at which Isaiah 6:10 was quoted is in Acts 28:26–28 where, it would appear, Paul turned from his countrymen to a more intensive ministry to the Gentiles. Paul, like Christ, quotes the text in full, upbraiding his listeners for closing their eyes to avoid understanding. Both Christ Himself and His servant Paul lay the blame for unbelief with the *unbelievers themselves*. [5] Let us turn to the OT passage itself. Read Isaiah 6:9-10.

CAL: In the AV it reads: "And He said, Go, and tell this people, Hear ye indeed, but understand not; and see ye indeed, but perceive not. Make the heart of this people fat, and make their ears heavy, and shut their eyes; lest they see with their eyes, and hear with their ears, and understand with their heart, and convert and be healed." That's not quite the same as the New Testament quotations of the passage.

JAY: "Make the heart of this people fat..." God's word to the prophet is in the imperative. We might express it thus: "Render them the more hardened by your warnings." Our Lord's quotation of the text however, shows that the people had closed their own eyes (Matt 13:15). Paul makes the same point when he quotes the portion in Acts 28:27. Now let us return to Isaiah, please.

Before Isaiah "saw His glory" there was this situation: the prophet in chapter one had given God's case against sinful Judah and this was followed by entreaty. "Come now and let us reason together saith the Lord: though your sins be as scarlet they shall be as white as snow." After entreaty and warning there is the Song of the Vineyard. What more could God have done for them? So it is asked. And with what result? "He looked for justice, but behold oppression; for righteousness, but behold a cry." And so, in 5:24 we learn that judgement is pronounced against sinful Judah "because they have cast away the law of the Lord of hosts and despised the Word of the Holy One of Israel." Therefore, the words of Isaiah 6:10 are given to the prophet to announce. The people had, in fact, conditioned themselves. They had in wilful disobedience despised God's Word. So 'judicial hardening' as you call it, is not to be viewed as something which God deliberately planned, to make faith impossible for those who desire to believe. It is rather the answer which He gives to those who persistently refuse to heed His Word. Are you following me?

CAL: I am. Is there not here the fact of the Hebrew idiom which we discussed in connection with the hardening of Pharaoh; the way of thought which conceives that what God foresees is going to happen as though it is inevitable?

JAY: Some do see it that way. But let's return to John. He sees a parallel with the situation in Isaiah's day and his own. Now although Isaiah's message was first of all for his own times, the New Testament writers recognise it as prophetic, and so apply it. Consider therefore John's record, in chapter eleven for background first, back to the raising of Lazarus. Many believed after witnessing that miracle, *but* some went their way to the Pharisees. With what result? The Pharisees gathered a council. 'What can we do?' they ask, "For this man doeth many miracles," they continue. They acknowledge that. They could not fail to acknowledge that. Rather than believe, they say: "If we let him alone all men will believe on him." And ought that not to have been wonderful and desirable? Not for them. Note their concern: "And the Romans shall come and take away both our place and our nation." That referred primarily to temple and nation perhaps, but also to the fact that they loved their place of authority and position of honour. The Lord had recognised this attitude in them, and so He had said: "How can ye believe which receive honour one of another, and seek not the honour that cometh from God only?" (John 5:44). So we reach the stage when John records, "But though He had done so many miracles before them, *yet* they believed not on Him."

CAL: Strangely enough however, John adds: "Nevertheless among the chief rulers also many believed on Him." Is that not like a contradiction?

JAY: There are two different opinions about those words. One view is that John uses the phrase to indicate full belief, and from this viewpoint, such believers are regarded by some as secret disciples, like Nicodemus and Joseph of Arimathea. There is the alternative view expressed by Bishop Westcott who says: 'This complete intellectual faith is really the climax of unbelief.'

CAL: Which do you believe?

JAY: I think Westcott was right, but I can't be sure. John's 'Nevertheless' would seem to favour the view that they were true believers. But it is written: "For with the heart man believeth unto righteousness and with the mouth confession is made unto salvation." Then we have our Lord's own words in Matthew 10:32-33, "Whosoever therefore shall confess me before men him will I confess also before my Father who is in heaven. But whosoever shall deny me before men, him will I also deny before my Father who is in heaven." We find a similar thought in Mark 8:38 about those who are ashamed of Him and His words. Now these chief rulers did not confess Him, and we may wonder how John knew that they 'believed.' We might perhaps ask, were they present at the unjust trial of Jesus? Were they deliberate absentees leaving only a quorum to condemn the Lord and to prosecute the case against Him before Pilate? Where were they at Pentecost and the Ascension? Were they absent when Stephen was martyred? We do not know. So, although I cannot be certain, I find it hard to resist the conclusion that their belief was not a saving trust in Jesus as their Saviour and Messiah. There was no allegiance. It may have been that some did later come out into the open, like Nicodemus and Joseph of Arimathea. We do know from Acts 6:7 that a large number of priests became obedient to the faith. Beyond that I cannot go.

CAL: The 'blindness' in this context would be a blindness to the meaning of the prophecies of the old covenant, to the Messiahship of Jesus. Paul makes it clear too in 2 Cor 3:14–16: that this lack of insight – this blindness – does not remove the individual's responsibility in the matter. Do you agree with me?

JAY: The basic lack in their lives was not insight – it was repentance! When any of them repents, the Scriptures make clear, when anyone turns to God, then the Lord will remove the veil, and enlightenment will follow. The cure for blindness is repentance. The same principles apply today. The Bible tells us to repent and believe. If we repent then God will help us to see and to believe in His Son.

CAL: So then the blindness of Israel was not part of God's plan?

JAY: God did not make it impossible for Israel to believe, if that is what you mean. But mere men cannot thwart God's ultimate purposes. He overrules, and the stubborn resistance of a Pharaoh, the treachery of a Judas, and the unbelief of the many are brought into the outworking of His plan. Out of that unbelief of the Jews 'arises the mystery of that Sacrifice which is to redeem the world'. But not as a contingency plan! Never think that, for the Lamb of God to whom the Baptist pointed at the Jordan is the Lamb of God *from before the foundation of the world.*

CAL: This discussion is helping me very much. I am left with 1 Peter 2:8. Let me read from verse seven for continuity: "Unto you therefore which believe he is precious: but unto them which are disobedient, the stone which the builders disallowed, the same is made the head of the corner, and a stone of stumbling, and a rock of offence, even to them who stumble at the word, being disobedient: whereunto also they were appointed." Those last five words are a difficulty to my understanding: "Whereunto also they were appointed."

JAY: Peter envisages two classes of people here: believers and unbelievers. How may they be distinguished? By their attitude to Christ. He is, so to speak, the Divine Touchstone. On the one hand are believers who hold Him in honour. To them He is precious. (Peter's word here actually has a fuller meaning than that. They 'share' in Christ's preciousness; they have a part in His honour.) On the other hand are the unbelievers. As builders might reject a stone, and leave it aside to be stumbled over, someone once said, so Christ is to them a stone of stumbling and a rock of offence. The thought is deeper than that. Christ to them is a stone of stumbling and a rock of offence, but why is this so, and what is the appointment? J.B. Phillips translates the verse thus: "Yes, they stumble at the Word of God, for in their hearts they are unwilling to obey it – which makes stumbling a foregone conclusion." And that I think expresses the truth of it very simply.

CAL: So, here too, those unbelievers, the disobedient ones, were not *appointed* or *destined* to unbelief?

JAY: Certainly not. We must reject all such fatalistic notions. "God would have all men to be saved and come to a knowledge of the truth" (1 Tim. 2:4). That is God's Word. What is then appointed? Not their lack of faith, but the *result* of their unbelief. Stumbling is the consequence of their disobedience. It is that consequence which is their sad destiny. 'Final impenitence will result in final rejection', but remember, the clear teaching of Scripture is that repentance will always meet with God's gracious favour. The 'broken-off' branches, if they turn from their unbelief, can be grafted in again, says Paul (Rom 11:23). Those who stumble at Christ can, by repentance, find in Him no longer the Rock of offence, no longer the Stone of stumbling, but the very Rock of Ages, the precious living Stone, whose life will make them living stones too. He will then be 'precious' to them in every sense. But that will do us for this discussion!

NOTES

1. See Campbell Morgan on this passage: *The Gospel according to Matthew.*
2 See Tasker on Matt. 13:35. p.139, and p.136 for Hoskyns ref.
3. Campbell Morgan p.73 (Matt. 7:6).
4. Pickering Commentary on John 12:39 (quoting Temple).
5. For deeper treatment of this see F. & M. p.195f and their whole Section 20, p. 189 *et seq.*

Determinism and Free Will

JAY: Have you come to discuss more problem texts, or are there other matters on your mind?

CAL: It's the general question of determinism that concerns me, and why people hold such opposing opinions when they are faced with the same evidence.

JAY: Why people differ in their opinions is a big subject, and we can discuss it later. What is the immediate issue for you?

CAL: I am thinking of DNA and genetic inheritance. Some scientists, though not all, maintain that our genes control everything, to the extent that there is no such thing as free will. Have you read about this, or shall I explain what I'm talking about?

JAY: I am only a layman, but I have read a bit on the subject, ever since Crick and Watson described the theoretical helical structure for the DNA molecule. DNA, as I understand it, is the substance that transmits genetic characteristics from one generation to the next. Would that do as a starting point for what you have to say?

CAL: It would indeed, For Dr Crick is one of the determinists, as I call them. He once said in an interview : 'You, your joys and your sorrows, your memories and ambitions, your sense of personal identity and free will, are in fact no more than the behaviour of a vast assembly of nerve cells and their associated molecules.'

But I could never accept that idea. If we were to carry his thesis to its logical conclusion, then there could not really be such faculties as reason and judgement, or logic and consistency. They would all be equally illusory. If Dr Crick is correct, his suppositions lose their validity because they are no more the result of reason than the plodding mindless orbit of the earth around the sun. [1] If he were right, then you and I would be no better than pieces of electronic equipment! What do you think?

JAY: Dr Crick is a famous scientist, but he is wrong in his deterministic philosophy about DNA and genes, in which he has gone beyond his science. I was interested to read some remarks which Stephen J. Gould made when he was writing about intelligence. He wrote: 'Biologists know that 'heritable' does not mean 'inevitable'. Genes do not make specific bits and pieces of a body: they code for a range of forms under an array of environmental conditions. Moreover, even when a trait has been built and set, environmental intervention may still modify inherited defects. The claim that inherited IQ is so many per cent 'inheritable' does not conflict with the belief that enriched education can increase what we call intelligence.' [2]

CAL: That's right. Genes do not rigidly define a trait, but define 'a reaction range' of probabilities of traits or behaviours developing. What I mean is, genetic inheritance endows each person with a range of *probable* physical or behavioural expressions. [3]

JAY: I was also very interested to read recently a lecture given by Professor Francis Collins, Director of the Human Genome Project in the U.S. This project is considered by some to be the most significant scientific project instigated in the 20th century. Professor Collins is a Christian, and he is an authority on DNA. He said: 'We talk about the heredity component as if that is all there is. Let us not forget free will. Some scientists seem to be embarked upon the notion of getting rid of that. We as Christians should resist that with our last breath.' [4] His whole lecture is most interesting, but I thought this particular passage might interest you.

CAL: I think it is very important, coming from an authority of his standing. There is a lot of nonsense talked about genes nowadays, such as the 'violence' gene, the 'compassion' gene, the 'homosexual' gene, and so on, and the media seize on terms like that. Scientists who are determinists claim that our DNA genetic code gives us no freedom at all. But the theological determinists also have their own rigid DNA code. 'Decreed: No Alternative'. For the Elect that would mean 'Destined: No Alternative'. For the non-Elect it would be 'Doomed: No Alternative'. Would you agree?

JAY: Well, I haven't heard the Decretal theology described in DNA terms before! Yet I have to admit that what you say is true. I come back now to your opening problem of why people, when faced with the same evidence, can come to different conclusions. We have very briefly noted how scientists can differ. They are human, like the rest of us, and perhaps there is no such thing as scientific objectivity, or theological objectivity, for that matter. We respect the work of scientists. Their experiments and researches may be valid, it is true, but interpretation of the evidence is often influenced by factors in their personalities. One science historian is quoted as saying:
'Science ... is not so much concerned with truth as consensus. What counts as 'truth' is what scientists can agree to count as truth at any particular moment in time... Scientists are not really receptive, or not really open-minded, to any sorts of criticisms or any sorts of claims that actually are attacking some of the established parts of the (traditional) research paradigms.' [5]
And what is true of scientists is true of theologians too; the same human factors are at work. Let me expand here with some general remarks. Truth, in every sphere, has its obscurities, because life is a very complex affair. Complete objectivity is hard to attain, as we can see from the mass of conflicting opinions in art, philosophy, politics, religion and science...

CAL: ...The physicist Max Planck claimed that theories are never abandoned until their proponents are all dead - that science advances 'funeral by funeral' (quoted by Sir Martin Rees in his book '*Just Six Numbers*' p.10). But why is it that so many eminent men and women, some with well-trained and logical minds, fail to agree on matters of extreme importance?

JAY: Many philosophers and thinkers have wrestled with that problem. Roger Bacon, Vico, Kant and Francis Bacon come to mind. There is general agreement, I believe, that the limitations of language contribute to the problem. Language cannot adequately express our deepest feelings, nor can it accurately communicate the utmost searchings of human thought. That can be one barrier to understanding and consensus. Various other factors have been put forward, and I'll quote at random as many as I can remember. They are: pride of position; undue regard for established authorities and doctrines; the fear of ridicule, of being rejected by one's own establishment, of being branded as a heretic; the reluctance to confess ignorance; and the desire to conceal ignorance with a pretence of knowledge. Further, the desire to explain everything, and the urge to settle for one theory, can come into play. Prejudice, character, predisposition, upbringing, environment, culture, and the influence exercised over the understanding by the will and passions, are all factors that have been suggested. So we see that convictions do not primarily spring from reason or logic. The English philosopher Herbert Spencer said: 'Opinion is ultimately determined by the feelings and not by the intellect.' That may be an extreme view, but I think we have to admit that at least three factors are influential: those of temperament, training and education. One eminent scientist, Sir Fred Hoyle, has written: 'It is hard in later life to doubt those basic tenets of intellectual thought which all one's teachers have accepted without question... educational continuity makes it exceedingly difficult to change these patterns.' I don't want to quote him out of context, but he did indicate that he and his co-author were disturbed to discover how little attention is generally paid to fact and how much to myths and prejudice. [6]

CAL: May I butt in here? I am reminded of a passage of A.W. Tozer, though I can't recall the exact source of my note. He wrote: 'While we all pride ourselves that we draw our beliefs from Holy Scriptures, along those border lines where good men disagree, we may unconsciously take sides with our temperament. Cast of mind may easily determine our views when the Scriptures are not clear.' Wouldn't that agree with what you said about the human factors?

JAY: It would indeed. But before we turn to consider the failures of some theologians, let me mention a further important consideration. It is recognised by many learned people, both in science and theology, in different disciplines, that there are limitations in the human mind which restrict the paths to the acquisition of knowledge. This must be remembered when we try to understand the revelation of God in His Word. An old writer of the 19th century said: '...everything connected with the infinite God must, from the nature of the case, have some difficulties to finite minds like ours, and therefore, difficulties, if fairly considered, can form no objection to revealed truth.' [7]

So we can't expect to understand everything. Still, let's see how far we have progressed in our discussion. You brought up a number of 'proof texts,' and I countered these with another set of 'proof texts.' But ALL of Scripture must be taken into account. That is to say, we must honestly and fairly face all that God has revealed to us about Himself. To magnify any one attribute of God to the exclusion of another will lead to error, and has led to error down through the centuries. One writer highlights this in strong words, and I quote him at length. [8]

"All the more important practical doctrines of Christianity inevitably follow, and can easily be deduced from, the statement that God is our Father; whereas the systems of theology which have started from God's sovereignty, or omnipotence, or justice, have never reached His love. The only thing they have recognised under that name is so limited, so capricious and so unreasonable as to be altogether beneath contempt. Instead of representing God's tender mercies as 'over all His works,' they have made Him care only for a few simply that in order by them His own isolated 'glory' might be promoted." (p. 300). He then continues against the worst extremists.

"The Saviour has been injured far more by unconscious

misrepresentation than by any openly avowed hostility. He Himself foretold that there would arise false teachers, and that they would deceive many. His prophecy has been strangely, sadly fulfilled. All kinds of absurdities and blasphemies have been shouted forth by persons suffering under the mad delusion that they were preaching the gospel. There have been men calling themselves Christians who have said that the sweetest music of heaven would be the wailings of the lost in hell. There have been men calling themselves Christians, who have maintained that God created the vast majority of mankind for the express purpose of consigning them to everlasting flames, in order that He might be, as they strangely term it, glorified. There have been men calling themselves Christians whose religion has consisted in breaking on the wheel or burning at the stake those who differed in doctrine from themselves. There have been men calling themselves Christians who have asserted that the grossest sins they might please to commit, after what they dignified with the name of conversion, would be matters of the most perfect indifference. There have been men calling themselves Christians who were remarkable for nothing save the conceited ignorance of the bigot, the childish puerilities of the formalist, or the sickening cant of the hypocrite. Now so long as anyone believes that such men are the genuine representatives of the teaching of Christ, he cannot be censured for refusing to call himself a Christian." (p. 321f)

CAL: That is a shocking statement! It's almost incredible, and yet, if we look back through the centuries, we have to admit its truth. Even if the persecution of Christians by others calling themselves Christians does not happen now, there are still deep divisions, especially in connection with the sovereignty of God. Isn't that so?

JAY: It is. All Christians acknowledge that God is sovereign, but there are those who understand the sovereignty of God in a way which not only negates the revelations of God's goodness and love, but denies free will. 'How can God be sovereign, yet grant free will to men?' they ask.

A.W. Tozer somewhere has said in this connection: 'If in His absolute freedom God has willed to give man limited freedom, who is there to stay His hand or to say, What doest Thou? Man's will is free because God is sovereign. A God less than sovereign could not bestow moral freedom on His creatures. He would be afraid to do so.' [9]

Can you accept that?

CAL: Oh yes. Completely. But I confess I am a bit hazy in my thinking on election and predestination in relation to determinism. I wish I could be clear about that.

JAY: Let's leave that for another meeting. Think over this discussion, and remember the saying attributed to St Bernard: 'Where there is not free will, there is nothing to save. Where there is not free grace, there is nothing to save with!'

NOTES

1. This is mostly from a letter by Mark Adkins in *Scientific American* (August 1992), p. 5. But see *The Astonishing Scientific Search for the Soul,* p.3, by Francis Crick (Simon and Schuster).

2. Quoted in the *Reader's Digest A-Z Book of the Body,* p. 65.

3. Warren S. Brown and Malcolm A. Jeeves in *Science and Christian Belief* (Vol. 11, no. 2, Oct. 1999. p. 143).

4. p. 101 of above. (*Science and Christian Belief*).

5. See p. 47 '*Creation*' magazine vol. 21 no. 4 1999. I add here some quotations from Halton Arp, an experienced astronomer, a recognized expert observer of quasars and galaxies, whose observations led him to put forward the view that redshifts are not caused by the expansion of the universe. His theory is unpopular with the 'establishment', and he has written of the censorship of unpopular ideas. However, he writes also of how the educational

process trains a scientist in what to think, rather than to think independently or creatively, and adds: "I gloomily came to the conclusion that if you take a highly intelligent person and give them (sic) the best possible elite education, then you will most likely wind up with an academic who is completely impervious to reality..." When looking at this picture, no amount of advanced education can substitute for good judgement, in fact it would undoubtedly be an impediment." pp. 131, 163 of *Seeing Red: Redshifts, Cosmology and Academic Science*, by Halton Arp (Aperion, Montreal, Canada,1999). This I took from a review of the book in the Technical Journal of *Answers in Genesis* vol. 14 (no.3) 2000.

6. See pp. 137 and 147 of *Evolution from Space*, by Fred Hoyle and N.C. Wickramasinghe (J.M.Dent and Sons London 1981).

7. See p. 66 *Sermons on The Second Advent of the Lord Jesus Christ*, Rev. Hugh McNeile (J. Hatchard and Son, Picadilly. 1842).

8. *The Origin of Evil* and other sermons by Alfred Williams Momerie (William Blackwood and Sons. Edinburgh and London. 1894)

9. *The Knowledge of the Holy*, p 18; A W Tozer (Send the Light Trust, Bromley, Kent)

Predestination and Election

CAL: All we have talked about so far has shown me that the Word of God does not support the doctrine (what I would call the fatalistic doctrine) of 'election to salvation', with its correlative term of 'election to damnation'. Some theological systems teach that, don't they?

JAY: They do, but beware of 'systems'. Remember the Bible is not a book of 'Systematic Theology'. A synthetic digest of doctrine nowhere appears in it. God Himself is not an intellectual system: He is a Person, the One with whom we have to do. We must not underestimate the importance of correct doctrine, but the foundation of our salvation is based on *our relationship with a living Saviour*, not on the acceptance of a creed alone. Furthermore, the man who wants to frame a complete system for human beings, in politics or religion, has to leave out important factors which do not suit his theory. For instance, if we turn from religion to economics for an illustration, Adam Smith has written: 'The man of system...seems to imagine that he can arrange the different members of a great society with as much ease as the hand arranges the different pieces on a chessboard. He does not consider that the pieces on a chessboard have no other principle of motion besides that which the hand impresses on them; but that, in the great chessboard of human society, every single piece has a principle of motion of its own, altogether different from that which the legislature might choose to impress upon it.' [1] We can apply that criticism to the theological systems which deny free will.

CAL: I see the force of your illustration. God is all-powerful, but

He does not view us as mere chess pieces, so to speak (nor as clay pots, as we have seen). Yet, since this is true, does it not raise the problem of contingency? By that I mean the problem of events being contingent upon - dependent upon - how men and women exercise their God-given power to obey or disobey?

JAY: Yes, it does. Dr Garbett, in his book *The Divine Plan of Revelation* has written of that as follows (p. 190f): 'During the whole course of God's revealed dealings with mankind, each successive transaction has been adapted to the circumstances of human conduct as they arose. There is no exception to this beyond the first sovereign act of the Divine will, which freely elected to enter into relations with man at all. All the subsequent actions were conditioned by the circumstances to which they were adapted. Thus, in regard to the whole design, the character of revelation, as a scheme of saving mercy, arose out of the fall of man. The special atonement accomplished by the death of the Son of God arose from the position of condemnation in which sin placed man towards the Divine justice. Thus, in particular instances, the sentence which condemned the Hebrews to wander for 40 years in the wilderness, arose from their disobedience in refusing to enter upon the possession of Canaan. The 70 years captivity in Babylon arose from the idolatry of Judah, and its special duration from their neglect of their Sabbaths. The same adaptation of God's dealings to the circumstances of man's action is to be traced everywhere. And yet, side by side with this pliancy and adaptation, there stands the absolute foreknowledge which comprehended each and all of these contingent variations within the limits of the same consistent plan.'
Does that long quote help you?

CAL: It reinforces my own thoughts on the subject. I was reading 2 Peter 3:12 recently in the AV which says: "Looking for and hasting UNTO the coming of the day of God," but the margin says - "hastening the coming". Is that correct?

JAY: It *is* correct. The NEB translates the same passage thus: "Look eagerly for the coming of the day of God and work to hasten it on." Sidlow Baxter comments on the verse: 'Read it just as

Peter wrote it, Looking for and hastening the coming of the Day. There is a co-operativeness between God's purposes and His people's responses. There is a certain contingency about our Lord's return.'

This world is a place of moral probation, and God works through human agents, always in harmony with morality. Hence we read of God delaying His judgement when we repent. In short, there is the possible change in the course of history, dependent somehow on human action. While God must be actively aware of all possibilities and can neither be surprised nor have His purposes ultimately frustrated, yet this contingency is real. Those last few sentences may need further explanation, but perhaps they are enough at this stage.

CAL: I can follow your thought. We did see earlier how Nineveh was spared when the people repented, and how God responds to the moral response of a nation. It is not that God changes His mind. He knows all things, and He knows the reaction of every human heart. It is rather His dealings with people which change, according to their obedience or disobedience. But He is in control. He overrules for the accomplishment of His ultimate purposes. So it happened that, in spite of all the failures of His chosen people, as recorded in the OT, the promised Messiah came "in the fullness of time". That purpose could not fail. You pointed out in an earlier discussion that our Lord Jesus Christ is the Lamb of God foreordained before the foundation of the world. The cross was in the eternal plan of God, and neither men nor the powers of darkness could possibly frustrate the accomplishment of the Divine plan of Redemption.

JAY: What a great truth that is! Our finite minds can not encompass the vast sweep of that Divine plan of Redemption for the universe: we grasp by faith what is revealed. But at this stage let us note that God's purpose in creation, His eternal purpose (Eph. 3:11), is revealed in Scripture as working to its end by the method of election. The idea of election is progressively unfolded in the history and prophecy of the OT (see HDB article on Election).

So let us consider what is revealed about predestination and election in the Scriptures. Some people do not differentiate between the two terms. However, they do not have the same meaning, in my opinion.

CAL: What is the difference between them?

JAY: Predestination is concerned with a Christian's FUTURE destiny. It is *not* about who should *become* Christians. It is not about that at all. It is rather that God has predestinated His people to be holy (Eph. 1:4); to be related to Him as sons (Eph. 1:5), and to be conformed to the image of His Son. Election is rather different. 'If to the idea of predestination you add that of election, you may find the teaching of Scripture to be that some are elect in order that through them others may be blessed. When God chose Abraham He certainly had this purpose in mind (Gen. 12:3b), and what was true of Abraham is true also of Abraham's spiritual seed. This is rather different from a widespread impression which has it that some are elect and the rest without more ado consigned to perdition.' [2]

CAL: I have read that the Greek word which is translated 'elect' means 'picked out' or 'selected'.

JAY: Primarily, that is so. But there is more than that to the word. It is used in different contexts in Scripture. It is used of:-
1. Christ, the Chosen One of God, as Messiah;
2. the whole nation of Israel;
3. believers within the nation of Israel (the election of grace);
4. the twelve disciples (apostles);
5. the Church in Christ;
6. the elect angels (chosen for special tasks in the Divine administration), and, I may add, the word is used even of Gentile kings.

CAL: Obviously then, and I keep pressing this point, election can't merely mean being chosen to go to heaven or hell, as you have already indicated. But please continue.

JAY: Let us begin with the twelve disciples, the apostles. Please read Luke 6:12,13.

CAL: "He (the Lord) went out into the mountain to pray. And when it was day, He called His disciples, and He chose from them twelve, whom He also named apostles." That tells us that Jesus selected only twelve men from amongst His many disciples, but as the others were still His disciples, then it is clear that the 'election' or choice of the twelve had nothing to do with either going to heaven or hell. The others who were not appointed were not 'reprobated' or disparaged. Do you agree?

JAY: Certainly I do. This election involved the bestowal of an office, the giving of a task. But the disciples' own wishes played no part in it, in that they could not appoint themselves to the office. Indeed, Jesus did tell the twelve, "Ye have not chosen me; I have chosen you." Their task was to witness to the life and resurrection of Jesus. So: there are two aspects of this bestowal of an office which we must note. In one, a man's will is involved, and over the other it has no control. God assigns the callings according to His will and foreknowledge. He is the Author of election. The office and the task to fulfil were ordained by the Lord alone. The Twelve were chosen. But what was NOT ordained was how they would match up to the task which He had allotted them. They could not do anything in their own strength of course, but if they were willing, God would supply the power to fulfil the task.

CAL: Judas was one of the Twelve, yet he fell from God's chosen office for him (Acts 1:17-25).

JAY: A terrible fall indeed. Election is an office, a responsibility, and a privilege. It is never an irresistible selection for the final blessing which obedience would receive.

CAL: Now what about the election of Israel?

JAY: Yes: here are some thoughts on that. The election of Israel, unlike that of the apostles, was of a corporate body; not the election of individuals. By being born into the nation, individuals were born into its election, an election which was like that of the Apostles in that it was unearned and unmerited, as we read in Deut. 7:7-8. God chose Israel alone from all the nations. From the nation would come the promised Messiah. The nation's task was to prepare the way for Messiah to bless the world, and then to 'arise and shine' with Him. So again it was an election to *service* rather than *salvation*.

CAL: So the choice of a nation did not determine the final destiny of individuals; it had nothing to do with whether they went to heaven or hell. Is that what you mean?

JAY: That's how I understand it. The nation would serve its purpose of preparing for Christ even if the majority of individuals belonging to it fell away from God's purpose for them. Their election was purely a matter of God's grace, and could be forfeited through unfaithfulness to its conditions. We see these two factors converging in election: the Divine will, and the nation's conformity to it. The LORD is a moral ruler and deals with the elect (as with all) in accordance with moral principles, the eternal principles of His own nature.

CAL: You said that by being born into the nation, individuals were born into its election. But that wasn't the only way for a person to enter that election, was it? Proselytes could do so. I am thinking particularly of Ruth. To Naomi she said, "Thy people shall be my people, and thy God my God" (Ruth 1:16). It was her own choice to become a convert to the Jewish faith and nation, and in entering the nation she entered also its election. Isn't that right?

JAY: It is. Indeed we see this clearly from the fact that she became the great-grandmother of King David, and so was an ancestress of the Lord Jesus Himself (Ruth 4:22 and Luke 3:23-32). We have seen that the election of the whole nation, as announced to Abraham, had the object of preparing a seed (Christ) through whom all nations would be blessed. Ruth, although she entered the election of the nation by choice and not by birth, partook of that election so completely as to become part of the line of descent to that seed. She was not chosen to become part of the nation of Israel, as you have observed; rather, in becoming part of that nation *she entered its chosenness.* I have recapped somewhat here, because I want to point out that there were certain INDIVIDUALS connected with Israel who were chosen for special roles, and indeed, in order to create Israel, God chose Abraham, Isaac and Jacob (see Neh. 9:7; Rom. 9:7, 13). He further chose Moses (Ps. 106:23) and David (Ps. 78:70), and, I should have said, Aaron, as the first high priest...

CAL: ...He even chose certain Gentile rulers, Cyrus, for example. But what about the election of believers within the elect nation of Israel – the 'election of grace' concept?

JAY: We noticed earlier that the nation of Israel could serve its purpose even if the majority of the individuals belonging to it fell away from God's purpose for them. Those who did so, those who did not live up to the task implied by their chosenness, lost the blessing which God intended for them. In Paul's day, this was largely true of the Jewish nation; they had failed to 'arise and shine' when the light of Messiah came to them. So Paul was led then to write of the truth about the remnant, in Rom. 9:27-29. Of this C.H. Dodd wrote (p. 172): ... 'that only a minority of historic Israel is to form part of the chosen people of God is distinctly taught in Isaiah's well-known doctrine of the remnant. (Isa. 10:20-23)'. ("It is the remnant that shall be saved," Paul writes.)

Bruce however comments: 'But IF ONLY a remnant will survive, AT LEAST a remnant will survive *and constitute the hope of restoration'.* Paul applies Isaiah's doctrine to the religious situation of his own day: there is a believing remnant through whom God in His grace will work out His purposes, because their faith is in Him and not in their own works. They had no merit in themselves. They had repented; they were now living by faith in God, and they are now what Paul calls the 'elect according to grace'.

That is only a sketchy answer to your question. I repeat that the

Divine plan of redemption will move on to its fulfilment in spite of any human failure.

CAL: My next question is about the angels. Paul writes to Timothy (1 Tim. 5:21) as if we were being watched by the 'elect angels'. The Bible tells us that there are fallen and unfallen angels, and speaks of thrones, dominions, powers, and principalities among them. Would it be right to say that the elect angels are the obedient loyal ones who did not follow Satan in his rebellion?

JAY: I feel sure they would all be included in the term 'elect', but, as you did mention, there seem to be certain orders or grades among them (and this would be so among the fallen ones too). Amongst the unfallen angels some are chosen perhaps for high executive office, with God-given authority. We read of cherubim and seraphim, and there are two references to archangels, only one of whom is named, and that is Michael. The only other angel whose name is given in Scripture is Gabriel, and he seems to be the bearer of tidings, revealing things. I think of him going to Daniel with revelations of history, to Zacharias to reveal that he was to be the father of John, the forerunner of Christ, and then to Mary to reveal that she was to be the virgin mother of the Saviour of mankind. Michael however appears to be especially involved in the war against the powers of darkness. He overcame the evil Satanic prince of Persia who hindered Gabriel's visit to Daniel, and we read in Rev. 12:7 of war in heaven, when Michael and his angels defeated the dragon and his angels so that the latter had no more place in heaven.

As for your remark about being watched by the elect angels, we are not merely being seen by them: we are 'watched over' by them.

CAL: "...The angel of the Lord encampeth round about them that fear Him, and delivereth them." Is that what you mean?

JAY: Yes, and I have in mind also Heb. 1:14 : "Are not all angels ministering spirits, sent to serve those who will inherit salvation?" Let me add that Daniel gives the angels - or some of them - the title "Watchers", and Peter says that even angels long to look into the mysteries of redemption, if I may put it like that (1 Pet. 1:12). We shall never know in this life what watchful care the angels exercise over the saints of God in every circumstance of their earthly pilgrimage.

CAL: I suppose we are too much like Elisha's servant (2 Kings 6:17) who saw only the threatening enemy forces until God opened his eyes to see the hills full of the divine protecting forces. So I deduce that the angels then are chosen (elected) to carry out special tasks in administrative association with God, and very much on our behalf. They are invisible, yet ever present. The truth is both comforting and sobering to me: 'watched over', but observed!

JAY: I can agree with you in all that.

CAL: I mentioned earlier that the Greek word for 'elect' could mean 'chosen', 'picked out', or 'selected'. But how can this be so when we think of Christ, the chosen One of God, as Messiah? He is unique, the eternal Son of God who became Jesus of Nazareth. There could be no thought of 'selection' as we think of Him. That's a great difficulty for me.

JAY: The difficulty arises because of the inadequacy of human language to express all that is contained in the Greek word for 'elect' or 'chosen' in the different contexts where it is used. (The difficulty is not confined to the Greek language. There is a simple but definite association of meaning in English - and indeed in Hebrew also - between the concepts of 'chosen' and 'choice'). It can have various meanings such as: choice, excellent, pre-eminent, or beloved. I'll try to illustrate this language difficulty with three examples from the Old Testament.

You probably know that during the last three centuries BC, the Hebrew Scriptures were translated into Greek to serve the needs of those Greek-speaking Jews outside the land of Israel who were no longer able to read their Scriptures in the original Hebrew. This Greek translation is known as the Septuagint (the LXX), and it became the Bible for the early Christian church. There are many quotations from it in the New Testament.

Firstly, let us look at Ex. 30:23, where we have the expression "pure myrrh" (AV). The RV here gives "flowing myrrh," and the Jerusalem Bible renders it "liquid myrrh". Now how can this be? Strong's Concordance for the (AV) word 'pure' states that is from an unused root (meaning 'to move rapidly'): freedom, hence spontaneity of outflow, and so 'clear', 'pure'. The Septuagint here uses the Greek word for 'chosen'.

The second illustration is from 1 Chron. 7:40, which reads: "All these were the children of Asher, heads of their fathers' house, *choice* and mighty men of valour, chief of the princes". The Septuagint here again translates 'choice' by the Greek word for 'chosen'.

For the third illustration let us look at S.o.S. 6:9. "She is the only one of her mother; she is the *choice* one of her that bare her" (AV). It is interesting to see how other translators have rendered that in English. The Jerusalem Bible uses 'favourite' for 'choice one', and Moffat uses 'my spotless one'. Strong, in his concordance, says that the Hebrew word for 'choice' in its various senses can mean: beloved, choice, pure, clear, clean. In this third example the Septuagint once more uses the Greek word for 'chosen'.

Are you clear on this so far, Cal?

CAL: Yes, I think so. Those three examples from the Old Testament do help to make clear what you said about the use of the Greek word for 'chosen', where the emphasis is on the *value placed* on what is described as 'chosen', rather than on the act of selection.

JAY: I would like you to be quite clear about that. Forster and Marston, in their important book *God's Strategy in Human History,* deal at length with this aspect of 'chosen'. After dwelling on

Messiah's task (to which we must return), they write: 'But there is more than that to the thought of Christ and election, there is rather the thought of His 'belovedness' to God, of His preciousness to God. We may gain some idea of this if we realise the close connection between 'eklektos' (chosen) and 'agapetos' (beloved) in reference to Christ. This is shown most clearly in the way in which the Gospel writers translate into the Greek language the words which God spoke (presumably in the Aramaic language) during the transfiguration of Christ. Matthew renders it: "This is my beloved (agapetos) Son, in whom I am well pleased: hear ye Him." Mark is similar: "This is my beloved (agapetos) Son: hear Him." Luke however renders the same words using the Greek word for 'chosen' (Luke 9:35 RV). "This is my Son, my Chosen (eklelegmenos): hear Him." (The AV gives 'beloved' here, but see WE Vine et al. The most authentic mss. give 'chosen'.) We see then that when the word 'elect' or 'chosen' is applied to Christ, its primary meaning is not one of selection but of *belovedness*.

'The point may be illustrated further from Matthew's rendering of Isa. 42:1. The Hebrew of Isaiah runs: "Behold my Servant, whom I uphold: my chosen, in whom my soul delights." The LXX quite naturally renders the word 'chosen' by 'eklektos', but Matthew does not follow the LXX in this instance. Instead, he renders the Hebrew using the Greek word 'agapetos' (beloved) thus: "Behold my Servant, whom I have chosen; my beloved (agapetos) in whom my soul is well pleased." Matthew therefore uses the word 'beloved' as a substitute for the word 'chosen' in this context (Matt. 12:18).

'This type of interpretation of the word 'chosen' is not unlike that of the LXX itself when it speaks of 'choice silver' (Prov. 8:19) or describes a beautiful girl as 'choice as the sun'. (S.o.S. 6:10, where the LXX uses 'eklektos' in a free rendering of a Hebrew word meaning 'pure' or 'clear'.) The emphasis is NOT on selection, but on the value set on the object described' [3].

That's a very long quotation, but I hope it helps you to understand this concept of 'election' when applied to Jesus as the Messiah, the Christ.

CAL: Yes, it does, and there are two verses in the New Testament which seem to me to reinforce the concept. Do you remember when I raised my difficulty with 1 Peter 2:8? I was not then thinking of the election of Jesus Christ, but it occurs to me now that verses 4 and 6 both support what you have been bringing before me. Verse 4 speaks of the living stone, rejected by men but "chosen of God and precious to Him"; and so does verse 6: "See, I lay a stone in Zion, a chosen and precious cornerstone". Peter here links the election of Christ to His preciousness to God: chosen and precious.

JAY: Yes, I think those two references from the apostle Peter do reinforce our understanding of the term 'chosen' when it refers to Christ.

CAL: You mentioned Messiah's task. Can we consider that now?

JAY: Certainly. But how do I begin such a great subject? We read in Phil. 2 of the self-humbling of the eternal Son of God. He did not come to be served, but to serve, to be God's chosen suffering Servant for the redemption of the peoples, and to destroy the works of the Devil; to be the chosen Servant who would be a light to the Gentiles. The first of Messiah's tasks is to bring back Jacob and gather Israel unto God (Isa. 49:5). His second task is stated in this way: "I will also give you for a light to the Gentiles, that you may be my salvation unto the ends of the earth." (Isa. 49:6. See also Luke 2:32.) I emphasise that He is God's suffering Servant, for His chosenness does not mean that He is given an easy time whilst others suffer. Rather, He himself is in the thick of the battle...

CAL: ...in the thick of the battle? What do you mean?

JAY: When we were speaking about the elect angels, we saw how Scripture indicated that there are thrones, principalities and powers both in the angelic kingdom of light and in the Satanic kingdom of darkness. When they were created by God, all the

81

angels were good. Some of them, however fell from their celestial position through the misuse of their free will. God made nothing evil. The evil spirits were not created demons, but became demons by a free act, and by that free act they cut themselves off from their Creator. Having dwelt in the presence of God, they have no doubt as to His Being and sovereignty. Yet ever since their deposition by God, they have been anti-God in all their activities. They tremble before God, but they do not love Him. Indeed, they are waging a relentless battle against Christ, and that brings me to the election of the Church. The Church – composed of individuals - is elect because it is IN CHRIST; and He is the Elect One, so the Church as part of His body is engaged in the war between the evil forces of the kingdom of darkness and the forces of the kingdom of light. We learn from Paul (Eph. 6:12) that "we wrestle not against flesh and blood, but against principalities, against powers, against the rulers of the darkness of this world, against spiritual wickedness in high places", or, as the NIV renders that last phrase, "against the spiritual forces of evil in the heavenly realms". So he exhorts us to put on the whole armour of God. Being chosen in Christ involves a call to battle, and implies that we are to fight in Messiah's armour...

CAL: ...Is that a reference to Isaiah 59:17? "For He put on righteousness as a breastplate, and an helmet of salvation upon His head?"

JAY: That seems to be the OT reference, and Paul details the 'armour of God' in Eph. 6:11-17 in which we must fight, and stand... [4]

CAL: ...Each of us must "endure hardness as a good soldier" in that battle. Is this our calling, our vocation, and God's chosen task for us in Christ? Paul says that after doing everything we are still "to stand". Isn't that endurance?

JAY: I am going to digress in response to what you have just said about "standing". In 2 Samuel 23 we have a record of David's mighty men. I mention two of them only. Eleazar "stood his ground" when the men of Israel had retreated, and God wrought a mighty victory after that stand. The second one was Shammah (v. 11f). Israel's troops again fled, but Shammah "took his stand" and again the Lord gave a great victory through His valiant warrior. There is a lesson for us in that, but I want to make a further point. Those great warriors could *see* the enemy arrayed against them. Now think of Job. He could not see his real enemy. Campbell Morgan wrote of that (p. 54 of *This Was His Faith*): 'God wasn't dealing with Job, but permitting him, even though at the time Job didn't realise it, to be an instrument through whom He was answering the Devil's lie. This is a big subject...but Job was really working with God, even though he did not know it at that time.'

Our great enemy, likewise, is invisible. Here lies many a perplexity. We must always remember that we are expected to maintain our stand when it seems there is nothing more we can do.

CAL: "Be thou faithful unto death," the Lord said to His persecuted church.

JAY: That's a solemn charge. But let me refer once more to Forster and Marston (p. 103f): 'We have seen how the words of Isaiah 49 apply to Messiah, describing His task as to 'bring back Israel' and to act as 'a light to the Gentiles'. We know that the Church also has to act as the light of the world just as Christ is 'the light of the world' (compare Matt. 5:14 with John 8:12). We will not therefore be surprised to find Paul and Barnabas applying the words of Isaiah 49 (about being a light to the Gentiles) to their own task as part of Christ's body the Church (Acts 13:47 quotes the LXX of Isaiah 49:6). They have taken up the task of the chosen One of God, *for they are part of his body and share in his chosenness.*" Are you clear on this so far?

CAL: Being 'in Christ' is a tremendous concept, but it is becoming clearer to me as we go on. You said that the Church is elect because it is 'in Christ' and He is the Elect One...

JAY: Yes, but notice one thing. The Bible does not say that we are chosen *to be put into Christ.* It says that we were chosen IN CHRIST. *Our* election is not separate from *His* election.

CAL: We are 'accepted *in* the Beloved', in Christ. Eph. 1:6 is the verse I have in mind: "To the praise of the glory of His grace, wherein He hath made us accepted in the Beloved."

JAY: That is the great truth. Let us consider it more fully. In Ephesians chapter one Paul outlines what I call 'God's glorious destiny for the Church':
1. we have been blessed with all spiritual blessings *in Christ*;
2. we have been chosen *in Christ*;
3. we have been favoured with God's grace *in Christ*, as you have just pointed out;
4. we have received redemption and forgiveness *in Christ*;
5. we have received an inheritance and a guarantee of that inheritance *in Christ*;
and if we go further into the epistle, we are seated 'in the heavenlies' *in Christ* (2:6); Jews and Gentiles have received a unity of reconciliation *in Christ* (2:13); and we have now boldness and access to God with confidence *in Christ* (3:12).

CAL: I am almost overcome at the wonder of it all. That God should choose creatures like us for such high destiny! But Paul reveals to us, in 1 Cor. 1:27f, "that God hath chosen the foolish things of the world to confound the wise; and God hath chosen the weak things of the world to confound the things which are mighty; and base (or lowly) things of the world, and things which are despised, hath God chosen - that no flesh should glory in His presence." It is a great mystery.

JAY: It is staggering. But, as I often say, faith can accept what our mortal minds can't grasp. Paul writes (Eph. 3:9f) of "the fellowship of the mystery, which from the beginning of the world hath been hid in God, who created all things by Jesus Christ: to the intent that now unto the principalities and powers in the heavenly places might be known by the church the manifold wisdom of God".

Perhaps it's time to draw our lengthy discussion to a close, but we do so with wonder and worship, as we contemplate the fact that we are to live and reign with Christ, and that at the final revelation of the sons of God, who have been conformed to the likeness of His Son, the whole creation, which has been groaning in travail, will be released from its present bondage.

CAL: Yes, and then all will be headed up in Christ. Every knee shall bow and every tongue confess that Jesus Christ is Lord to the glory of God the Father. Oh glory! Hallelujah! I'm lost for words.

But thank you very much for going into these things with me so fully. My mind is now clear of the determinism of a creed which denies free will in the realm of morality, and which denies human responsibility.

JAY: I'm glad that you feel helped in this way, and I'm sure that you now realise how vital it is for us to exercise that God-given responsibility to walk according to His holy will at all times. So let me end this discussion with the sobering words of Peter (2 Peter 1:10f) to give diligence to make our calling and election sure, and this is done by the constant cultivation of the Christian graces which he has just listed in detail. He is not here referring to a choice between heaven or hell. Heaven will not be a classless society, as various Scriptures might seem to indicate (especially 1 Cor. 3:10-15), and Peter's concern here is that we have a 'rich welcome', a 'triumphal entrance' into the eternal city. So Cal, with that prospect ahead of us, we obediently follow the Captain of our salvation and soldier on!

NOTES

1. Adam Smith in *The Theory of Moral Sentiments*, London, 1759; part 6 chapter 2, penultimate paragraph.
2. F.F. Bruce in *Answers to Questions*, p. 235.
3. Forster and Marston in *God's Strategy in Human History*, p. 101f.
4. Forster and Marston in *God's Strategy in Human History*, p. 103f (But see the whole Section on Predestination and Election in this very important book. I have freely referred to it in my essay.)

CONCLUSION

In approaching the subject of theological determinism, I realize that for many people it can have no interest at all. I have not written for them. I have in mind those Christian believers who may be disturbed by an erroneous doctrine which claims to be based on Scripture.

Christians should not belong to any school of thought, or hold any theory, which impugns the revealed character of our great God and Saviour. The revelation given to us is that God is love (1 John 4:8); God is light, and in Him is no darkness at all (1 John 1:5); He is the God of all grace (1 Peter 5:10); He is the Father of compassion, and the God of all comfort (2 Cor. 1:3). He hates sin, but loves the sinner. He desires that all men should be saved, and come to a knowledge of the truth (1 Tim. 2:4).

It is necessary to remember that the Word of God is not given to us so that we may try to formulate correct theories. It is given to us so that we may have the truth.

The question may then be asked, since there are divergent interpretations, how are we to know what is truth? The short answer to that question is: by obedience to the will of God. On that, I must write more fully.

The Lord Jesus said (John 7:17), "If anyone chooses to do God's will, he will find out whether my teaching comes from God, or whether I speak on my own." Campbell Morgan comments on that text: 'The attitude of the soul for the detection of final authority is that of **willing** to do God's will. When men are completely consecrated to the will of God, and want to do that above everything else, then they find out that Christ's teaching is Divine, it is the teaching of God.' I quote also from an earlier writer, F W Robertson. On March 2nd 1851, he preached on John 7:17, and entitled his sermon, *'Obedience the organ of spiritual knowledge'*. In his sermon he said that 'the witness of the Spirit of God in man is to be realized, not through the cultivation of the intellect, but by the loving obedience of the heart'.

However, to know the truth is not necessarily to understand it. There are truths reaching far beyond the comprehension of finite minds, because there is nothing exactly corresponding with them in the whole sphere of human knowledge, as, for example, the Trinity of Persons in the unity of the Divine Being. Paul writes (Phil. 4:7), of the peace of God *which passeth understanding.* In Eph. 3:19 he writes of knowing the love of Christ *which passeth knowledge*, and to the Corinthians (1 Cor. 13:12), he says that now we see in a glass darkly (or, 'in a riddle'). It is *by faith* that we understand; the Holy Spirit "searches all things, yea the deep things of God", and reveals to the believing heart what the mind of natural man cannot conceive. But humble, loving obedience always plays a part in any advance in spiritual wisdom and understanding.

It was so in Old Testament times too. I think of Moses addressing the children of Israel (Deut. 4:6), where he speaks of the God-given commandments. "Keep therefore and *do them,* for this is your wisdom and understanding". In Deuteronomy 29:29 we read: "The secret things belong unto the LORD our God: but those things which are revealed belong unto us and to our children for ever, that *we may do* all the words of the law". All obedience was to be rendered in love for God. The command in Deuteronomy 6:5, "And thou shalt love the LORD thy God with all thine heart, and with all thy soul, and with all thy might", is repeated several times in that book. But all had to be done in faith. When we read in Deuteronomy 32:20 of a generation which had provoked the Lord, He described them as "children in whom is no faith".

William Kelly, in his *Lectures on the Pentateuch* (p. 497), says:

'I have no doubt at all that when we weigh Scripture, we shall in due time see the wisdom of it all. But it is not a question of how far we can appreciate the wisdom of God. Our business is to believe and obey Him... The simplest child of God may follow and be subject to His word.'

I end by quoting a verse of a hymn, with which I trust all my readers will agree:

> *"How good is the God we adore,*
> *Our faithful unchangeable Friend,*
> **Whose love is as great as His power,**
> *And knows neither measure nor end."*

Glory be to His name. Amen, and Amen!

Scripture Index

Isaiah		**10:32,33**	58
6:9,10	56,57	10:37	22
10:20-23	76	11:28	19
37:26	24	12:18	80
42:1	80	chap. 13	56
45:7	24	13:10-17	49
45:9	45	13:15	57
45:22	15	13:35	51
49:5,6	81	23:37	46
chap. 49	83	26:28	13
55:7	24,27		
59:17	82	**Mark**	
		4:10-12	54
Jeremiah		4:12	48,49
18:4-6	40	8:38	59
18:7-10	34	14:24	13
18:11	41		
chap.19	40	**Luke**	
26:3,13	34	2:32	81
27:13	45	3:23-32	75
		6:12,13	74
Ezekiel		7:30	45
chap. 18	29,30	9:35	80
33:11	24	14:26	22
		chap. 16	44
Jonah		22:20	13
4:2	34		
		John	
Habakkuk		1:29	14
3:17-19	43	2:17	28
		3:16	14
Malachi		3:17,18	12
1:2f	23	5:16	53
		5:38,42	54
		5:40	48
Matthew		5:44	58
5:14	83	5:45-47	54
6:24	22	6:44	48
7:6	52,54		

Hebrews		**3:9**	14
2:9	15	3:12	71

1st Peter		**1st John**	
1:12	77	1:5	86
2:4-6	81	2:2	15
2:8	60,81	4:8	86
5:10	86	4:14,15	15

2nd Peter		**Revelation**	
1:10f	85	3:20	46
2:22	53	12:7	77
		22:17	19

Names Index

BOOK LIST

Baxter, J. Sidlow   *Explore the Book* (one vol).
                                     Commentary on the Bible.
                                     Zondervan Publishing House, Grand
                                     Rapids, Michigan 1975

Blaiklock, E.M.   *Commentary on the New Testament.*
                                     Hodder and Stoughton, London 1977

Bruce, F.F.   *Answers to Questions.* The
                                     Paternoster Press, Exeter, 1972

Cole, Alan R.   *Exodus: An Introduction and
                                     Commentary.* Tyndale OT
                                     Commentaries. The Tyndale Press,
                                     London 1973

Dodd, C.H.   *Commentary on Romans.* Collins,
                                     Fontana Books

Ellison, H.L.   *Ezekiel: The Man and His Message.*
                                     The Paternoster Press, Exeter 1956

Forster and Marston   *God's Strategy in Human History.*
                                     Send The Light Trust Bromley, Kent,
                                     1973 ed. (USA edition by Tyndale
                                     House Publishers inc., Wheaton,
                                     Illinois 1974)

Garbett, Edward   *The Divine Plan of Revelation.* Boyle
                                     Lectures for 1863, London. Hamilton,
                                     Adams and Co. Paternoster Row,
                                     1864

Hoyle, Fred and N.C.
Wickramasinghe   *Evolution from Space.* J.M.Dent and
                                     Sons, London, 1981

McNeile, Hugh   *Sermons on the Second Advent of
                                     the Lord Jesus Christ.* J. Hatchard
                                     and Sons, Piccadilly 1842

Momerie, Alfred Williams   *The Origin of Evil* and other
                                     sermons. William Blackwood and
                                     Sons, Edinburgh and London,1894

Morgan, G. Campbell   *The Acts of the Apostles.* Pickering
                                     and Inglis Ltd. London, 1965

	This Was His Faith. (Expository Letters) Compiled and edited by Jill Morgan; Pickering and Inglis, London
	The Gospel According to Matthew, and *The Gospel According to John.* Marshall, Morgan and Scott, London, 1976 ed.
	Searchlights from the Word. Marshall, Morgan and Scott, London 1976
Pinnock, Clark H. (Ed).	*Grace Unlimited.* Bethany House Publishers, Minneapolis, Minnesota USA 1975
Rees, Martin	*Just Six Numbers,* Phoenix 2000, Orion House, London
Smith, Adam	*The Theory of Moral Sentiments,* London 1759
Tasker R.V.G.	*Matthew: An Introduction and Commentary.* Tyndale NT Commentaries. The Tyndale Press, London 1971

Books, journals, magazines and reference works not listed above:

The Technical Journal of CREATION, Vol. 14 (no. 3) 2000, published by Answers in Genesis, Ltd., and printed by Triune Press, Brisbane, Australia

Creation magazine, Vol. 21 (no. 4), 1999, published by Answers in Genesis, PO Box 5262, Leicester, LE2 3XU

The Reader's Digest A-Z of the Human Body, published by The Reader's Digest Association Limited, 25, Berkeley Square, London, WIX 6AB 1987

Science and Christian Belief, Vol. 11 (2) October, 1999. Printed in Great Britain for Paternoster Periodicals, PO BOX 300, Carlisle, Cumbria, by Polestar Wheatons Ltd., Exeter

Scientific American magazine, August 1992 issue.